T0194877

INSIGHTS TO
FINDING
Spiritual
PEACE

Short Bible Studies and Teachings That
Help You Recognize and Benefit from the
Work of the Holy Spirit in Your Life

LEX ADAMS

WESTBOW
PRESS®
A DIVISION OF THOMAS NELSON
& ZONDERVAN

WestBow Press books may be ordered through booksellers or by contacting:

WestBow Press
A Division of Thomas Nelson & Zondervan
1663 Liberty Drive
Bloomington, IN 47403
www.westbowpress.com
844-714-3454

Scripture taken from the King James Version of the Bible.

"Scripture quotations are from the ESV® Bible (The Holy Bible, English Standard Version®), copyright © 2001 by Crossway, a publishing ministry of Good News Publishers. Used by permission. All rights reserved."

Scripture taken from the Amplified Bible, Copyright © 1954, 1958, 1962, 1964, 1965, 1987 by The Lockman Foundation. Used with permission.

ISBN: 978-1-6642-5391-9 (sc)
ISBN: 978-1-6642-5390-2 (hc)
ISBN: 978-1-6642-5392-6 (e)

Library of Congress Control Number: 2021925664

Print information available on the last page.

WestBow Press rev. date: 02/08/2022

INTRODUCTION

As each day of our life unfolds, it brings with it varied opportunities and challenges. We cannot control what each day brings. However, we can be assured there are divine, eternal purposes in each new day. Our peace and contentment are fulfilled as we discover what they are.

The secrets of the Lord's purposes are found in the Bible. It is as the Holy Spirit opens our eyes to His Word that we gain His insight. It is then we can say, "I understand."

The chapters of this book represent the "now I understand" moments which the Spirit of God used to comfort and establish my own heart. The answers always come from Him. His Word is the one source for them all. He is faithful to meet the seeker.

This is not a book to be read through quickly, but rather each chapter is a Bible study or commentary which should be contemplated prayerfully. To receive the greatest benefit, have your Bible with you are read the referenced Scriptures. Approach this book as individual studies, and allow time to dig into the content.

As a writer of words, I cannot give you any spiritual insight. I am powerless to cause the words in this book to bless, enlighten or strengthen you. I can only pray that the Holy Spirit will anoint them and bring them to life for you in a way that will benefit your walk with God.

May the Spirit of God bless your heart with the fullness of His understanding. He is the only teacher. He is the giver of comfort, wisdom, understanding and strength. He is the One who does a wonderful work in the heart of each believer. To Him alone be all the praise, honor, and glory.

WHAT WE SEE IN JESUS IS GOD'S WORD

Heavenly Father, we come to You in need. We look to and wait upon You for our help and deliverance. We have no sufficiency of ourselves to sustain us through the storms of life. The challenges we face reveal this to us. It is our pride that would tell us otherwise. We will never grow from the place of reliance upon You, and in fact it is in growth that we realize how fully we need You. Thank You for helping us understand that through difficulty we are drawn to You as our only source of strength, comfort, encouragement, and peace. Thank You for Your faithfulness toward us, and Your never-ending mercy which reaches us in every moment of need. Your Word is a sure foundation of hope and promise, and it is upon this Word we shall stand, by faith. Praise be to You alone! In Jesus's name we pray. Amen.

THE WORD BECOMES FLESH!

John 1, tells us that the Son of God, Jesus, was the Word - the divine communication of God Himself through the Son. All that God is and has spoken is manifest in Jesus, the Word manifest in the flesh (John 1:14). We see in Jesus the intentions of God for humankind. Jesus is the final outreach of the Father's heart for his "created likenesses" (you and me) to acknowledge Him and His love for them. Jesus, the Word, is God framing speech in not only words alone, but in demonstration and physical manifestation. Jesus is God's finest effort at communication with man. God is saying, not only will I speak to you, but I will show you Myself, and live among you in flesh, to make clear my desire for your acceptance of My love and care for you.

Our Lord's sacrifice is beyond adequate expression. The magnificence of His death and resurrection, and the mystery of His atoning blood, are the hallmarks of God's manifest love. And in His life among us, we see the unshakable integrity of God's Word, through His touch and His spoken words and actions. We see how great a confidence we can place in the Word of God - a confidence we are directed toward as a source of enlightenment, nourishment and sustaining power in our daily lives. The Word was manifest in the flesh visibly, so that we might place our trust in the invisible Word or things of the Spirit; that we might lean upon it in every circumstance; that our faith would be cemented permanently to an unwavering trust in the Word of God.

We see in Jesus that God reached out and touched all who came to Him, and who released faith in Him and His spoken words. The blind men who received their sight relied upon His touch and His word as sufficient to heal them (Matt. 9:27-30). The bleeding woman reached out to touch the Word, knowing by faith she would find healing in Him (Matt. 9:20). The centurion asked only that Jesus speak the word, and he believed that his servant would be healed - and he was (Matt. 8). We see in these accounts of Jesus's life that, with confidence, men and women reached out to Him, placed trust in what He said, and received the loving touch of God upon their requests.

And now to us - to us who have no physical manifestation to look upon. To us, who have the printed Word, and the Holy Spirit. We who look upon an empty manger in which, long ago, a Holy Child lay. Where do we go in our hour of need? Which street of the city is Jesus walking down now when we need to find Him...to be touched by Him... to hear Him command healing and peace over our lives? Where is He residing this evening, that we might knock upon the door and say, "We would desire to see Jesus?" At which table is He seated for His evening meal, that we might take up a chair next to Him and lay our weary head upon His chest and feel the warmth of comfort, the great power of knowing that in His presence all is taken care of and we can hear Him say, "Be at rest, I will take your burden"? Where is He just now? For we need to find the sweet release that comes from speaking our needs and burdens in His ears and looking into His all-knowing eyes as His presence frees us from the bondage of fear and anxiety of oh, so many things.

He is here! He is in our hearts by His Spirit. He is manifest to us in His Word. For the printed Word is the very living Word that was manifest so long ago. It is His Spirit that quickens it to our hearts by faith in a way that brings us into His presence, just as if we were following Him down the streets of old. We can touch His garment today! We can hear Him say "according to your faith be it done unto you." We can feel His touch, and look into His eyes, as the Spirit makes real to us … the Word. We can rely upon the written Word as confidently as others relied upon His physical touch and audible voice. We are no less the object of His care and affection than those who saw Him in the flesh. His Word is of no less power to us than it was to them. We, with them, share in the same privilege of belonging to Him. And we can partake of the fullness of His blessings as we, by faith, proclaim that we will stand upon His Word - which is indeed God, the Word who was in the beginning with God (John 1:1).

If there is a continuing blessing in the remembrance of His birth the first Christmas, it is in knowing that His presence is continuing, eternal, and accessible to us today. All that God manifests in the life of Jesus - His love, comfort, forgiveness, healing, deliverance, hope, encouragement, compassion, mercy - are yet there for us today through our faith in His Word.

Do we go there with expectancy and faith? Do we walk the pages and read the verses as those who sought Him in the streets of the towns and villages of years ago? Knowing that when we find Him, we will receive from Him that which we need? Do we allow the Holy Spirit to quicken to our hearts the reality of His presence through the written Word? Do we believe that the Word, through the power of the Holy Spirit, is today waiting to minister to us the touch of God, just as Jesus touched so many when he walked this earth in the flesh?

It stands true today that those who seek Him in such a way will indeed find Him to be the same as the centurion found Him, as the blind men found Him, and as the bleeding woman found Him. He is the same, yesterday, today, and forever! The Word we read is the Word manifest in the flesh - the living God, waiting for us to receive Him as such. Reach out by faith and touch Him in your moment of need. Reach for Him in His Word. Expect Him to be found of your heart as you seek Him down the pages and verses of life, the pages, and verses of the Word. Place your trust unshakably in His Word and He will uphold you. He will never fail you. See Him there - on the path just in front of you! He has stopped and is standing still, commanding that you come to Him. He has heard your cry just as he heard Bartimaeus (Mark 10:46). He is in that verse of promise with His hand outstretched. Take it! His touch is for you, today.

UNYIELDING THOUGHT PATTERNS, ROBBERS OF GOD'S BLESSING

Heavenly Father, we seek Your face to learn to know You better. We are comforted by the life found in Your Word. We are nourished by its truth. Our minds are con formed a little more to Your ways each time we ponder the wonders of the Bible. Your message to us is one of love, forgiveness, restoration, and life. While we deserve none of these, yet we are grateful for Your care and great love toward us. Open our understanding increasingly, for we see so very little. We have no offerings to give You that are comparable to Your love and to Jesus's sacrifice. So, we come to give You our lives, our hearts, our wills, our days. Take them and make them meaningful to You, and somehow useful in the work of Your kingdom. Glorify Your wondrous name through our vessels of clay. In Jesus's name we pray. Amen.

A GLIMPSE INTO THE WAYS OF THE SPIRIT

The story of the healing of Naaman, the captain of the army of Syria, is an intriguing view of several aspects of the ways of God. Naaman was a leper. The story begins with a raid by Syria on Israel in which a young Israeli girl is captured and becomes a servant to Naaman's wife. Through this maid's testimony about God being able to heal leprosy, Naaman comes to the king of Israel with a letter from the king of Syria asking him to heal Naaman's leprosy. It started when the girl said, "Would God my lord (Naaman) were with the prophet that is in Samaria, for he would recover him of his leprosy" (II Kings 5:3). Naaman had responded with faith to the words of his wife's servant girl, prepared himself for the journey to Israel, and went expecting to be healed. This word of testimony from a captured slave girl was to turn a powerful leader in Syria into a believer in the living God.

When Naaman arrived in Israel to see the king, the king of Israel displayed no faith and was extremely threatened by the request to heal Naaman. How was the king supposed to heal him? The king must have thought that Syria was seeking to provoke a fight. The prophet Elisha responded with faith and confidence in God. Elisha sent to the king of Israel and said, "Wherefore hast thou rent thy clothes? Let him come now to me, and he shall know that there is a prophet in Israel" (II Kings 5:8). So Naaman went to Elisha.

Naaman was a man of war. He was a mighty man of great authority in the land of Syria. He arrived in front of Elisha's house with his horses, chariot, and servants. Presumptuously Naaman expected Elisha to greet him personally, after all he was an important commander of the Syrian army, and perform a dramatic act to heal him. Elisha did nothing of the sort. He quietly sent a messenger to speak to Naaman. He did not even come out to meet him. Elisha was not desirous of being acknowledged of himself, he was obeying God, and God was desirous of Naaman acknowledging Him, not Elisha. The messenger said to Naaman, "Go and wash in Jordan seven times, and thy flesh shall come again to thee, and thou shalt be clean." (II Kings 5:10)Naaman was enraged! He charged away in his chariot to leave in great anger. God and the prophet had not met Naaman's preconceived ideas. This was not how Naaman had envisioned being healed. He resisted God's direction because it seemed foreign to his own thinking. We read: "Naaman was wroth, and went away, and said, Behold, I thought he will surely come out to me, and stand, and call on the name of the Lord his God, and strike his hand over the place, and recover the leper. Are not Abana and Pharpar, rivers of Damascus, better than all the waters of Israel? May I not wash in them, and be clean? So, he turned and went away in a rage" (II Kings 5: 11-12). There is a great lesson in this error. We too easily turn from the guidance of the Spirit because we cannot fit it into our own thoughts and ways. Our pride can cause us to stumble at this point. We come perilously close to losing His blessing when we respond in this way.

After storming off in a rage, Naaman was approached by his servants who convinced him to do as the prophet had said. They reasoned with him and said, "If the prophet had bid thee do some great thing, wouldest thou not have done it? How much rather then when he saith to thee, wash, and be clean?" (II Kings 5:13) We then read that Naaman humbles himself and goes to the Jordan. Looking at the water, he must have wondered, "what difference will this make, it is only water?" It was humbling for him to step down from his chariot, disrobe, and submerse himself in the water, with his servants watching. It was not a great noble act. It was not "some great thing" as his servants had said. He stepped into the water once and got out. He repeated this seven times. It took faith to do this seven times. After the sixth time he looked at his flesh and he was still a leper. He could have stopped, but he did not. One more time he entered the water, and upon coming out he looked at his body. His servants were watching also, and there before his eyes his flesh turned clean and new again, like the flesh of a child. Imagine the feeling in Naaman's heart. He had obeyed, humbled himself, and overcome his pride and anger. He had stooped to submerse himself seven times in the river Jordan. He was cleansed and healed, no longer a leper.

Naaman then returned to Elisha and proclaimed, "Behold, now I know that there is no God in all the earth, but in Israel" (II Kings 5: 15). Further he said, "Thy servant will henceforth offer neither burnt offering, nor sacrifice unto other gods, but unto the Lord." Naaman had met God.

Elisha had handled the situation as God had required and not thrust himself between Naaman and the work God was doing in Naaman's heart. The Spirit had done the work from beginning to end. From the word of testimony from the captive slave girl to the instructions of Elisha, to the humbling of Naaman, and the healing of the leprosy, God had directed, and God was glorified. Thus, by allowing the Spirit to direct, many were blessed along the way. Naaman returned home a believer in the God of Israel. We are not told what effect this had upon those around him, but we do know that they saw him leave as a leper and return healed. This was known by all those around him in his home country, including the king of Syria. Jesus even references this healing as he addressed the unbelief in those to whom he was speaking in Nazareth (Luke 4:27). The power of faith and obedience is far-reaching. Whatever our role may be, may we seek to be obedient and responsive to the ways of His Spirit.

DO NOT GIVE UP BECAUSE OF THE APPEARANCE OF THINGS

Heavenly Father, we are grateful to You for Your love and care. We are awakened to the reality of Your presence daily, as we stop to consider how we are blessed. The power of Your Word is beyond compare! Its working in our lives is revealed in the most unlikely of situations, yes, in all situations. From all that is written, we are given a wealth of examples which we see unfolding within the setting of our own lives. There can be no doubt, You will never leave nor forsake us, for we see You manifest in our lives daily. In the difficult situations, in our testing, in our victories, in our uncertainty, we see You in them all, even if sometimes later than You would desire. Forgive us for our lack of faith, and our doubt which blinds us to the working of Your sacred hand in our life. Open our eyes anew to the wondrous presence of the Holy Spirit in each moment. For it is only as we trust You by faith, that we can walk in Your peace. In Jesus's name we pray. Amen.

THEY THAT BE WITH US ARE MORE THAN THEY THAT BE WITH THEM (II KINGS 6:16)

King David was a man confronted with many battles, challenges, and tribulations. His life was not one of quietude. In his old age he spoke a wonderful statement of his observations about God's care for his people. He spoke from a platform of a lifetime of experiences and relationship with

God. He said, "I have been young, and now am old; yet have I not seen the righteous forsaken, nor his seed begging bread" (Psalms 37:25). The righteous are not left alone, they have the companionship of God! The book of Hebrews confirms these words saying, "I will never leave thee, nor forsake thee" (Hebrews 13:5). This is absolute fact! God will not leave those who have been born again!

This promise is an anchor for our souls. Trials and difficulties will of necessity come. There will be a multitude of experiences we each will pass through. We will fight our own battles as did David. We will struggle to understand God's plan and purpose in the midst of many things. There are times when it will be hidden from us, for a season. This does not mean we are forsaken. This does not mean God has withdrawn His love for us. Faith must grow. Our trust in God must be blind to what surrounds us. We must know that our God is with us always. We must simply know this! And we learn to know this as David did, by looking back and seeing that we have been preserved through our past challenges. We have been sustained by His unseen hand which has brought us to this day. He has been there all along. God has answered prayer, sometimes slowly (by our judgement), sometimes rapidly. We can look back and see He has been there, behind the scenes, when at the current moment He looks invisible and seemingly distant. As our faith and trust are matured, we know without doubt that He is always there. We know He is there regardless of what we are facing.

There is a wonderful story, in II Kings chapter 6, of two men facing an overwhelming enemy. One had his eyes of faith open, the other did not, at first. Elisha was targeted by the king of Syria because he was warning the king of Israel of Syria's military strategy. God was telling Elisha what to tell the king of Israel for Israel's protection. Finally, the king of Syria found the city where Elisha and his servant were located. One night, the king of Syria's army surrounded the city. When Elisha's servant rose early in the morning and went outside, he saw the host of Syria surrounding the city with chariots, horses, and a great host. He returned to Elisha and said, "Alas, my master! how shall we do?" (II Kings 6:15) Alas indeed! What a hopeless looking situation. Where would they run? How could they escape? The appearance of the matter was disastrous.

Elisha answered his servant: "Fear not: for they that be with us are more than they that be with them." (II Kings 6:16) Where was this more of which Elisha spoke? The servant certainly did not see them. One man (Elisha) saw victory and resources to help, and his servant saw only the host of Syria standing against him and his master. The servant saw a hopeless situation. Elisha saw God! Elisha then prayed as we read in II Kings 6:17, "Lord, I pray thee, open his eyes, that he may see. And the Lord opened the eyes of the young man; and he saw: and behold, the mountain was full of horses and chariots of fire round about Elisha." God was there all the time, visible to Elisha, yet not visible to his servant until his eyes were opened in the spirit. Elisha then prayed for God to blind the entire army of Syria, which the Lord did. The balance of the story is rather humorous, as two men, Elisha and his servant, lead the entire army of Syria captive to the king of Israel. God delivered Elisha from this hopeless appearing situation because of his faith and trust in God.

Are we surrounded by an enemy army in our lives? Is there an attack being made upon us by Satanic forces? Is there a circle of hopelessness appearing to close us in? God is with us! Let us pray to see His help and let us trust and exercise our faith in His presence in our lives. These accounts of God's help are given to us for our edification and to sustain us in times of challenge. As we release our faith in God and His written Word, we will see the armies that assail us led away captive as God preserves us unto the day of His coming. And may the Lord help us to remember, that though the afflictions of the righteous may be many, He promises to deliver us from them all! (Psalms 34:19). Praise God!

FACE IT AND BE BLESSED ... WE HAVE NO EXCUSE FOR OUR SIN

Heavenly Father, we come before You once again and lay aside the guilt of our shortcomings and sin. We let go of it, for holding onto our guilt only separates us from You in our own minds. You stand ready to accept us always, even the instant after we falter, provided we confess our sins and place our hearts afresh beneath the cleansing blood of Jesus. It is Satan that would lie to us and deny us fellowship with You. Therefore, we come! We come in weakness. We come with imperfections. We come with pains and distress. We come not seeing all things clearly. But Father, we come! For in You alone are the answers, the comfort, and the words of eternal life. Work out in our daily lives Your purposes. Let us not be as the one who looks into Your face, but then turns to daily life forgetting what we are to be in You. Keep us in a walk in the Spirit, that our lives might be a light and encouragement to those around us. In Jesus's name we pray. Amen.

SO, THEN EVERY ONE OF US SHALL GIVE AN ACCOUNT OF HIMSELF (ROMANS 14:12)

Accountability of one's own life and actions is clearly defined in Scripture. The fact that there is a day of judgment in which each man will give an account and answer for his actions is also clear. "For we must all appear before the judgment seat of Christ; that everyone may receive the things done in his body, according to that he hath done, whether it be good or bad" (II Cor. 5:10). (See also Rev. 20: 12.) Romans 14: 12 makes a particularly important point about accountability. We will each give account of ourselves. We will not give account for the others who touch our lives. There is a school of thought which says, "people have problems because of how others have raised or treated them." This is true. A broken home can be the reason for juvenile crime and gangs. Abusive spouses can be the product of being raised in abusive homes. But if we don't get past these abuses, we give the person in the gang or the abusive spouse an excuse for their conduct. If this approach holds true of itself, then, on the day of judgment, the thief will say, "Lord, it is my parent's fault, for they divorced when I was young, and I therefore I got into trouble. Don't judge me for my actions, judge them for failing me." Scripture does not support this conclusion. The thief will be judged for stealing. The abusive spouse will be judged for his or her own actions, and the cause may or may not play a significant role in that judgement. Each person must choose their pathway, and choose what they will do going forward past abuse. Being a victim is not justification for sinful behavior. That may sound harsh, but we will look at what Scripture offers us on this subject in a moment. What is important is to ask, "what did the abused person do to get help?" "What did the abused person do to not follow in the steps of abusive behavior?" "Did the abused person take their pain and damage to the Lord for help?" Did the abused person choose to get help and avoid becoming an abuser themselves?

The root problem is not how we are raised or treated by others, nor what behavior we observe. The root problem is the fact we are born in sin. Our sinful nature will take us down one wrong road or another until we are yielded to God and transformed by the power of the indwelling Holy Spirit of God. The fact that wrong behavior by others affects us is true. But it is not a valid excuse for sinful behavior. Each parent will give an account of their works as parents. Each spouse will give account of how they treated their spouse. Each person will give an account of the example they were to others. Wrong actions by anyone will have an evil effect on others. This evil effect is not license for sin. God is able to transform any person who comes to Him. I do not speak to justify or minimize wrong actions. There is no doubt that they have a significant effect on other people. An abusive parent creates a very great challenge for any child to overcome. But whether our challenge is an abusive parent, an unfair employer, or wrongful imprisonment such as Joseph endured, we still must individually stand before Christ and answer for ourselves, what we have done with His message of salvation.

What has the troubled child done with the message of Jesus Christ? What has the ill-behaving individual done with the message of God's deliverance and transforming power? The purpose of this chapter is to strip us of all excuses. We have none! Yes, the road has been rough. Yes, we have been wronged. Yes, we could justify our behavior in our own eyes, and in the eyes of others as well. Yes, our parents, and we as parents, have made mistakes that affected us and others. Before God, we have no excuse. We are commanded to yield to Him and the work of His Spirit in our hearts (James 4:7-8, and Romans 12:1-2).

1 Peter 2:18-23 speaks beautifully to this issue. "Servants, be subject to your master with all fear; not only to the good and gentle, but also to the froward. (The unjust). For this is thankworthy, if a man for conscience toward God endure grief, suffering wrongfully. For what glory is it, if when ye be buffeted for your faults ye shall take it patiently: but if when ye do well and suffer for it, ye take it patiently, this is acceptable with God. For even hereunto were ye called: because Christ also suffered for us, leaving us an example, that ye should follow his steps. Who did no sin, neither was guile found in his mouth, who when he was reviled, reviled not again;

when he suffered, he threatened not; but committed himself to him that judgeth righteously."

The challenge is to accept accountability today for our own actions. Some of us may have faced greater obstacles than others to overcome, but regardless of the size of the unfair or cruel things that have touched us and shaped us, we must throw them aside as invalid excuses and today walk in the fear of God. "And if ye call on the Father, who without respect of persons judgeth according to every man's work, pass the time of your sojourning here in fear" (I Peter 1:17). God is able to heal and transform the vilest of human experience. Therefore, He has the right to judge without regard to persons. There is no favoritism in His judgement. The adulterous woman who came to Him was forgiven. There was no discussion of the reasons for her fallen lifestyle, simply the command to go and sin no more (John 8:3-11). The fallen nature of man is the problem, and the reasons we use to blame someone or something else for our improper behavior only hinders us from being transformed by the power of God. If His deliverance power was limited to only moderate difficulties, then perhaps some excuses would be valid. Thank God, this is not the case. He is able to save, deliver, and heal all who call upon His name.

Today, no matter where we find ourselves, here is a prayer we can pray. "Lord, regardless of the reasons I may lean on as justification for my sin, self-pity, depression, anger, or other improper behavior, I come to You, Lord, and admit I have no excuse. Heal me from my pain and suffering, Lord, and transform my life. I stand before You stripped of justification, confessing my sins, asking for Your touch. And if I have wronged others – my children, my spouse, my family, my friends or acquaintances - and been a bad example before them in my sin, forgive me. I lift their lives to You now. Into Your hands I commit them and look for Your Spirit and grace to cover them, heal them, and transform them in Your love. And today, let me live in Your Spirit. Today, let me be an example of Your grace and transforming power. Today, in the place I find myself, let my heart rejoice in You. Let me be kind to all who touch my life. And let me share Your love and light in all my words and actions."

We may never stand before multitudes in ministry. We may never do great exploits for God in the eyes of man, but let us have the grace of God to not fail in the common places of life in which He has placed us. May we have His insight to see the importance of being in Him for the benefit of those He chooses to place in our lives, particularly the importance of our family (I Tim 3:5).

THE ONLY PATH TO BLESSING ... THY WILL BE DONE

Heavenly Father, we seek You for the ability to always discern Your guidance. We are easily confused and often reject Your counsel. Help us to recognize Your voice more clearly. Looking back, we can see where mistakes were made, and for those we ask and accept Your forgiveness. As we go forward, may we be more sensitive to Your instruction and quicker to obey. Transform our thinking to be submissive to the Word and the Holy Spirit. May we learn to cherish obedience regardless of the cost, that You may make us a brighter light in this world and a help to others. In Jesus's name we pray. Amen.

OBEY, I BESEECH THEE, THE VOICE OF THE LORD... AND THY SOUL SHALL LIVE (JEREMIAH 38:20)

We are very much like Zedekiah and Israel. We have difficulty accepting the direction of the Lord and often do not understand it. Through the circumstances surrounding Israel, God was getting Zedekiah's attention, but He did not receive his obedience. In Jeremiah 38:14, Zedekiah brought the prophet Jeremiah to him to seek the counsel of God. Jeremiah told Zedekiah that he should yield to the king of Babylon and surrender. If he obeyed this word, then he and the city would be spared destruction (Jeremiah 38:17). This direction was certainly not easy to accept. Israel, the people who could say: "God called me; God delivered me; God established and blessed me," was now being told to surrender to the enemy or be destroyed. Go to Babylon? How could this be God's counsel? This leading of God seemed quite opposite the historic experience and the "God will bless me" attitude of Israel. When God had brought so many miraculous victories before, how could Israel surrender to the guidance Jeremiah proclaimed? Perhaps deliverance was coming from the seemingly hopeless situation and surrender would rob them of the victory. On its surface, the advice from God's prophet could be argued against sufficiently to be ignored.

Then there was Zedekiah's personal problem. He was afraid to obey Jeremiah's counsel. He feared that if he surrendered and was taken to Babylon, the Jews who had already been taken there would turn against him. (See Jeremiah 38: 19.) Fear of the possible reaction of others froze Zedekiah and prevented his obedience. God always controls what happens to the obedient person. Fear of what others may or may not do is never grounds for disobedience. Zedekiah's eyes were not upon the Lord, but upon people. This will always bring confusion and lead to wrong decisions. Pride and refusal to humble oneself under the hand of God is also a factor in spiritual error. For the king to surrender was the ultimate act of humility. God had pronounced the captivity of Israel for His own reasons in judgement of their sin and disobedience. It was not a time to stand upon historic experiences and preconceived notions of His leading. Zedekiah did not have the insight or strength to obey, and the price he paid was catastrophic. (See Jeremiah 39:6-8.) We too may pay a heavy price for not obeying the leading and guidance of the Lord. We should take this seriously.

Johanan failed in similar fashion to obey the voice of the Lord. He remained in the land after Zedekiah was taken and Jerusalem destroyed, but he feared that the leaders of Babylon would destroy him and the remnant of the people. (See Jeremiah chapter 41.) Johanan and the people with him had determined to enter Egypt for safety (41:17), which in the realm of natural thought could have been a good idea. Having just been invaded and destroyed, any other country would appear safer. Before going, Johanan and the people with him came to Jeremiah to enquire of the Lord. They swore to Jeremiah that whatever God told him they would do, even though they were already headed toward Egypt in their hearts (Jeremiah 42:3). God told them that if they would stay in the land, He would bless them. He addressed their fear of the king of Babylon and said to not fear him because God would deliver them out of his hand (Jeremiah, 42:10-12). In chapter 43 we see the sad rejection of God's words by Johanan and the people. They couldn't accept His advice because of the fear in their own hearts. Their eyes were upon Jerusalem's recent destruction and the apparent safety of Egypt, which God said would not be safe for them if they disobeyed. The very things they feared would befall them in Egypt. Obedience is our safe place!

Neither one of these examples is simple. There were many surrounding circumstances that made the guidance of the Spirit foreign to natural thought. Obedience is not always easy because of our inclination to rely upon our own reason. Having just witnessed the destruction of Jerusalem and the taking of the Jewish people into captivity, it would be difficult to accept staying in the land and expecting a blessing. The key to obedience is focus; focus upon the Lord, His word and His leading. Surrounding factors may be brought to Him in prayer, and all concerns and confusion that we may express to Him are not sin. We err when we do not take our concerns to God and then proceed away from the Spirit's leading. Zedekiah and Johanan would have prospered by continuing to reason with God about the advice received until they understood its value. Disobedience always carries with it a price that is not pleasant to pay.

Our goals, objectives and thinking must be surrendered to God. His work is different than we expect much of the time. We are inclined to look to the outcome of the "war", the condition of the "walls", and freedom from the constraints in our life as those things which are most important. God on the other hand looks upon the heart, and desires to accomplish His inner work of transformation. If we are placed on the losing side of the battle and are surrounded by burnt and destroyed walls while we are under the direction of a "foreign king", we will yet be victorious if we learn to obey God and His inner work is accomplished in our hearts (Jeremiah 29:11).

YOU ARE OF GREAT VALUE!

Heavenly Father, Your love comforts and encourages us in the place we find ourselves. Our refuge is not in a distant land, free from the current burdens upon us, but is in Your presence in the midst of where we live. Our value in life is not measured with the scale of earthly wealth and position, but by the scale of love hung on Calvary's cross. Jesus came to earth to purchase our salvation with the price of His life and His blood. He paid the same price for each soul who will believe, for each one is of great value in Your eyes. By the example of His lowly birth and humble living, we are taught the importance of inner matters of the heart and the temporal worth of all else in this world. Help us to keep our eyes upon Your ways and values in our own lives and in the lives of others. In Jesus's name we pray. Amen.

HAVE NOT... RESPECT OF PERSONS (JAMES 2:1)

In our own minds, with what do we clothe ourselves? How do we measure our value to God? Are we discouraged by our status in life? What clothing do we admire in others? Are we impressed by the outward appearance of success, position, moral correctness, or etiquette? It is our nature to be impressed with these things. It is our error to measure by them alone. Jesus seeks to help us place these things in the proper perspective. James speaks to the issue in the book of James, chapter 2, saying, "My brethren, have not the faith of our Lord Jesus Christ, the Lord of glory, with respect of persons. For if there come unto your assembly a man with a gold ring, in goodly apparel, and there come in also a poor man in vile raiment; and ye have respect to him that weareth the gay clothing, and say unto him, Sit thou here in a good place; and say to the poor, Stand thou there, or sit here under my footstool: are ye not then partial in yourselves, and are become judges of evil thoughts? Hearken, my beloved brethren, hath not God chosen the poor of this world rich in faith, and heirs of the kingdom which he hath promised to them that love him? But ye have despised the poor...if ye have respect to persons, ye commit sin, and are convinced of the law as transgressors." The world tends to blindly accept, respect, and place great value upon people in positions of authority, the rich and powerful, those with titles... God does not!

Our unregenerate nature thinks highly of those who appear to be successful. But if down the road an individual no longer holds a successful position, we tend to think less of them. We judge wrongly if we look only on the appearance or person of an individual. God sees and places value on each person equally and is not a respecter of persons (I Peter 1:17; Col. 3:25; Rom. 2:11). No one soul is more important to Him than another. While everyone is given varying responsibilities in life, our value does not vary with God. God uses positions of responsibility to teach those who need such an experience.

Lesser assignments in life are equally as important to God. Success in God's eyes is doing that which He has given with a heart attitude that is proper before Him (Col. 3:22-24). Our value in the sight of God is no greater if we are given much responsibility and it is no less if we are given little. Not everyone is given five talents (Matt. 25:14-15). Our acceptance is through faith in Jesus and His redemptive work on the cross. Our growth and reward is through obedience to Him. It is unwise to compare ourselves with another. How we perform in our individual circumstances is what is important. The harlot Rahab was justified in the eyes of God by her work of assisting Israel's messengers, and she was certainly not held in esteem by others (James 2:25).

Faith in Jesus is a great equalizer (James 1:9-10). The poor, the rich, the successful, the simple, the teacher, and the pupil, all must bow before the same throne of God. Hebrews 4:13 states, "... all things are naked and opened unto the eyes of him with whom we have to do." The only clothing which is accepted by the Lord is that which He gives through obedience to Him. The degree to which we are clothed with His likeness is a valid measurement, not our position nor the earthly circumstances He chooses to place us in to accomplish this goal. Through the humblest of surroundings our Lord came into this world. Through a life of rejection and ridicule he revealed the nature of God to a sinful people. Through the vilest of experiences being mocked, beaten, publicly humiliated, and crucified, He purchased our redemption.

It is wise for us to learn to see others, and ourselves, through the eyes of the Lord... of great value! We should not measure our success and worth, nor that of another, by that which is apparent, but by God's love shown us through Jesus. Responsibilities in life are given for a reason, and God teaches us to respect those in positions of authority and leadership (Romans 13: 1-7). Wisdom gives us the insight to discern if any outward success is coupled with inward rightness with God, and likewise, if any apparent humility is real or superficial. Lowly surroundings do not make one humble, nor does success make one proud. The attitude of the heart alone determines these matters.

ARE YOU IN GOD'S HIDDEN WORKSHOP?

Oh, Lord, our God, Your ways are truly wrapped in the word mystery. To our natural understanding we can call them by no other name. We do not comprehend for we have difficulty sitting at Your feet. Stillness and patience are not things we easily adopt. We strive for understanding and yet fall short of clarity, for our reasoning leads to confusion and doubt. We too easily miss the pathway of simplicity. We too heavily lean upon our own abilities to reason. We are too easily impressed by what our senses experience and too little controlled by an understanding of Your nature and holiness. We are bombarded with enormous amounts of the world, its ways, and its measurements. Protect us from such influence upon our perception of You and Your ways. Too much of what we see is mixed with unholy fire, and we are slow to discern for the dullness of our spiritual sight. Bring us to the simple and deep ways of the Spirit. Separate us unto Yourself fully, for the longing of our hearts is satisfied only by You. In Jesus's name we pray. Amen.

TWICE HIDDEN

There is normally a conspicuous absence of praise from and acceptance by the multitudes in the life of the one led by the Holy Spirit. Success in the religious world, as man measures success, is often missing from the life of the true saint. God has a way of hiding His own and hiding from them many of the beautiful things He does through them. Partly for our own protection, lest our ego rise to claim an ounce of glory for His working, and partly for our preparation. When there is a public moving of the Holy Spirit through a saint, there is normally an equal balance of persecution. Equal is not quite correct. The more Jesus ministered; the more opposition mounted against Him (John 10:31). The more Paul was used of the Spirit, the more time he spent in jail or fleeing for his life (Acts 9:23). Even with the public and open moving of His Spirit, the appearance of success, as we measure it, was not there (Luke 4:28-32). Opposition and persecution do aid in keeping folks humble. When, through our own energies, we move to "work the works of God", worldly success and admiration is more likely. (John 12:43).

God has a way of hiding us while He prepares us for His purposes. He does not accomplish this by placing us in remote seclusion geographically, but rather in the middle of our busy world. Isaiah 49:2 states, "in the shadow of his hand hath he hid me and made me a polished shaft." God brings His shadow over our lives in the place we find ourselves. While we are busy with daily life, God is busy polishing us to make us an effective witness for Him. Just as common cloth is used to polish fine jewelry, so the common cloth of life's experience is used by the Spirit to make us shine as a reflection of God's grace and Person. The cloth of challenge, adversity, heartbreak, sacrifice, and misunderstanding must be rubbed upon the tarnished areas of our life to bring forth the image and reflection of Jesus. When we find ourselves wondering why we are challenged on this issue or that, remember we are under His shadow for the purpose of refurbishment, rebuilding and transformation. We experience all the things common to man in our journey, but all things common are turned holy by the hand of Him who has placed us under His shadow. His hand is upon the common cloth.

And then again, He hides us! Isaiah 49:2 continues, "in his quiver hath he hid me." Sharpened, polished, prepared and then placed in his quiver. Hidden again to the outside world, we find God placing His polished arrows into his quiver. God is not interested in displaying His handiwork in us as a piece of art for public appreciation. This would build our religious ego to the point of destruction. He is interested in glorifying Jesus. It is in allowing God to keep us hidden that we find protection and usefulness. If we are not content to sit in His quiver, we are not fit to be placed in His bow. Being sharpened and polished is not license for self's energies to carry forward. If we strive to be the one holding the bow, we overstep our purpose. We must ever remain in His quiver until He places the bow string upon us. Without His hand upon the bow, even the most prepared arrow will miss the mark. Hidden for preparation and hidden for service... while contrary to natural thought, it is yet the glorious place to which our Lord calls us. Will we trust Him and rest in His shadow, and find contentment in His quiver? If we will, our service will carry the sharpness and power of His anointing when we find Him placing us in His bow.

A PURIFIED CHARACTER

Heavenly Father, Thou Holy One, we bow before the revelation of Your greatness and glory. The more we see and understand of You, the greater our sense of gratefulness, the keener our awareness of our need for You, and the quicker our knees bend to humble ourselves before You. We are more ignorant than knowing, and by Your grace we begin to see this. In the light of Your teaching us we bow...for it is Your light which reveals our need to be humbled. It is by Your grace and nearness that we learn to say, "I am the least." It is a good thing to be brought to that place where we say, "I know nothing of myself, Lord, teach me." From that place today we offer our praise, and the request for our eyes to be opened anew to the wonders of Your Word. We request of You to give us a teachable spirit... not an easy task for such a willful people. Thou art able, but we must first be willing. We pray to be brought to that place of inner submission and total abandonment to You, that we might know You, for this is Your desire for us. In Jesus's name we pray. Amen.

UNTO THE MEASURE OF THE STATURE OF THE FULNESS OF CHRIST (EPH. 4:13)

What is the ultimate intention of God for the Christian? Is it to make him active in Christian work? Is it to loosen him in the administration of the gifts of the Spirit? Is it to make him aggressive in evangelizing the world for Christ? The answer is none of the above. Character is the primary objective of God. The great I AM is interested in bringing us to be like Jesus. It is when we rearrange God's priorities that confusion enters the Church. Without first accomplishing the primary goal of being like Christ, then all other activities of Christian practice are tarnished with human nature and satanic influence. When Christian work is undertaken without character being established by the Holy Spirit, the level of expression is beneath the intentions of God. When evangelism, gifts of the Spirit and other Christian work are placed as the central theme of emphasis, they actually hinder the accomplishment of God's goal of character. Christian work and the expression of the Holy Spirit are the outflow of spiritual character and a mature relationship with God. They are the new wine which is preserved and served from new wineskins. Character is the new wineskin that must be in place before there can be the proper containing of the new wine of the Spirit.

Through the eyes of those who have not developed Godly character in Christ, the root source of expression of Christian activity is not discernable (Hebrews 5:14). Those who stand in positions of leadership, and do not focus on the development of character as the critical foundation, actually block the way and prevent others from entering the spiritual development God intends. Looking at the book of Isaiah we can see an example of the results when the ultimate goal of God (character) is bypassed for religious activity. In Isaiah 1:10-17, we see God rejecting the previously ordained sacrifices and service of the temple. The activity was taking place and to the immature eye it appeared proper, scriptural, and ordained of God. God saw it differently. He saw that holy character was missing. God's ultimate intention was bypassed for the lesser priority of religious activity. The result was religious service which God rejected. When instruction is out of line with God's priority of developing Godly character, then the substitute priority stands in the way of entering into the way of the Spirit. This is very similar to what Jesus said of the scribes and Pharisees in Matt. 23: 13: "But woe unto you, scribes and Pharisees, hypocrites! for ye shut up the kingdom of heaven against men: for ye neither go in yourselves, neither suffer ye them that are entering to go in." Those who sincerely desire to enter into a walk in the Spirit, which leads to development of character, are easily swept up into man's priorities and thus prevented from entering the pathway of God's priority.

Through the development of character comes the true perception of the awe-inspiring holiness of God. From an enlightened platform of relationship with Jesus, through the development of His character within the believer, the work and ministry of God are anointed, holy, and glorious. From the lower level of Christian activity, which bypasses character and relationship development, we find the holy things of God sinfully handled by untransformed humanity. This was the reason God rejected the offerings in Isaiah. Isaiah 29: 13 states this issue concisely: "Wherefore the Lord said, forasmuch as this people draw near me with their mouth, and with their lips do honour me, but have removed their heart far from me, and their fear toward me is taught by the precept of men..." Teaching or ministry which preempts character is the precept of man, not the Holy Spirit. New Testament service is also subject to God's wrathful rejection (Matt. 7:21-23).

Without Holy Spirit led teaching and character development, the motives of man and the influence and confusion of Satan permeate spiritual activity. Ridiculous practices are free to enter the activity of the Church and are a disgrace to the holiness of God, slandering the precious moving of His Holy Spirit. Immature hearts become the sidetracked seekers of the next new thing, the next mysterious supposed "move of God." In ignorance, those who lack relationship and character in Christ state, "I can't understand it, and it seems strange, but it must be of God for look at all the people affected; look at the Christians who participate in it. I felt so blessed." Brothers and sisters, there is much taking place in the realm of charismatic activity which is grossly out of order and not born of God's Holy Spirit. It is tantamount to taking the Ark of God out from the holy place and casting it into the marketplace of fallen man. Merely touching the Ark cost Uzzah his life (II Sam. 6:6-7); mishandling the holy things of the Spirit is no less of an offense to God. We need to be cautious lest we adopt the "attitude of the Athenians", who spent their time in nothing but to hear or tell some new thing (Acts 17:21). We are not to be "children, tossed to and fro, and carried about with *every* wind of doctrine" (Eph. 4:14).

Yielding to the secluded pathway of spiritual character development will bring the discernment and relationship with Jesus necessary to prevent deception in these last days. There is no other way to learn of Him and of His ways. As we learn to know Him, the imposter becomes very apparent. This is why the ministry of the church is to bring believers into the fullness of Christs' stature (Eph. 4:11-15). The moving of the Holy Spirit is never an embarrassment to God's majesty or holiness.

SALVATION IS ONLY
THE BEGINNING!

Heavenly Father, praise You, for you are worthy of our praise! Touch our eyes so that blindness and ignorance may fall from our understanding. Place a fire in our hearts to seek You and serve You. Burn away the dross of complacency and lukewarm seeking. Teach us to redeem the time by wisely spending our moments in prayer, praise, and yielding to You. When the day is done, may we look back and see that we have made time for those things which are important according to Your priorities, though other things are left undone. In Jesus's name we pray. Amen.

FOR THIS CAUSE, I BOW MY KNEES UNTO THE FATHER (EPH. 3:14)

Paul here expresses what he prayed for the Christians in Ephesus. His prayers are further explained in Ephesians 1:15-19. Paul begins in Eph. 1:15 saying, "after I heard of your faith in the Lord Jesus, and love unto all the saints." He was writing to Christian believers. This is important to recognize in properly grasping the fullness of the following passages. In verse 17, Paul prays that these Christians would be given the spirit of wisdom and revelation in the knowledge of the Lord. His next request of God is that the eyes of their understanding would be enlightened. One could suppose that their understanding was just fine, as they had already expressed their belief in Jesus. They could have easily stood and proclaimed, "Oh, yes, I understand all about salvation, I know Jesus as my personal Savior." Paul knew better; he knew there was much more to understand. Salvation was not the end, but rather the beginning of enlightened understanding. Understanding salvation is the first light, which is followed by continual enlightening as we seek and yield to God. Through wisdom and revelation from the Spirit, our understanding grows as we spend time in worship, in prayer, and in the reading of God's Word.

Paul then asks that they come to understand the hope of their calling. This hope must be more than salvation because the Ephesians had believed in Jesus and His salvation and at least understood that portion of the message! Paul wanted them to know about the riches of the glory of the inheritance of the saints. He also prayed for them to know the exceeding greatness of the power of God Who had saved them. He seems here to be searching for words which could begin to describe God's power by saying the "exceeding greatness" of His power. Explaining, as he moves into chapter two, that this great power that raised Jesus from the dead is the same power that quickened them to salvation. This mighty God who raised the battered, bruised, and dead body of Jesus to life, is the same God who has touched us and extends His power toward us as well. Indeed, it is this power that works in us! (See Ephesians 3:20.) Paul is praying they will see this truth and grow in it, not simply be satisfied to be saved and heaven bound. This Jesus, who is the head of all power and authority (above all other power or authority), is the head of the church, which is His body.

We then, as a part of that spiritual body of Christ, have His life power flowing in us. It is present in us. Just as blood flows to every cell of the human body, so God's power and Spirit flow to every member of His body. To the degree that we are enlightened to understand the magnitude of this, we discover limbs and functions active in us we never knew we had. This is what Paul is praying for. Paul knew that unbelief and limited enlightenment were like a tourniquet, which would keep the life of God from fully expressing through the Christian. Paul dramatizes his concern by saying he "bowed his knees before the Father." He was not merely praying but was getting down on his knees before God with this very important request. Paul knew that the flow of living water and power were full to the point of the faucet, which is the Christian. He wanted the Ephesian believers to learn, grow, and yield to the flow of this life, and not be found blocking it. He wanted the faucet fully open.

As Paul speaks in the third chapter of Ephesians, he is praying for the Christians to be strengthened in the inner man; that Christ would dwell in their hearts; that they would be rooted and grounded in love; and that they would comprehend the breadth, and length, and depth and height of the Christian experience. Salvation is not to be the waiting room for heaven. There is an entire world of spiritual life, experience, and growth for the Christian. Paul is praying that we would get out of the waiting room and discover and explore the greatness of life in Christ. It is as if we were invited into the entry hall of a great mansion. Some are content to just be in the mansion and desire to go no further. The entry hall is salvation, and that is good enough for some. However, this was not good enough for Paul, nor was it that for which he was praying. He desired that the Christian explore all the rooms and glorious grounds of the entire heavenly estate... now, while in this life. For the believer who knows something of God's love and salvation, Paul prays in chapter 3:19, that the believers would "know the love of Christ, which passeth knowledge, that ye might be filled with all the fullness of God." This requires moving from the entry halls of heaven into the many rooms of the spiritual mansion which is Christ's fullness.

Ephesians 3:17 finds Paul praying that "Christ may dwell in your hearts by faith." A strange thing to say to those who had received Him into their hearts, or so it seems. However, Paul's emphasis is focused on more than initially receiving Christ. Paul is saying, "You have received Christ into your hearts through salvation. I do not want you thinking that because you are now forgiven, you may proceed through life on your own plans. On the contrary, I pray for Christ to dwell fully and completely in all of your heart until you are full of the fullness of God." To dwell means to house permanently. This is more than an occasional yielding to or seeking of God. This does not mean a gaining and then losing of salvation, but rather a mindset that seeks to continually please God and yield to him, as compared to a casual faith in Christ while living for self-satisfaction. Paul wanted the Ephesian believers to allow Christ to dwell permanently in their lives, and this was his prayer. He did not want them filing their salvation away as one would an insurance policy but desired them to enter through salvation into the wonders and glories of God in the Spirit.

Through every experience in life, we will find growth and greater revelation from God as we understand the purpose of life and of our salvation. We must taste of the chastening, the discipline, the trials, the testing, the *love* and comfort of God in order to experience the fullness of Christ. He is in all of these experiences with us. We will see the glories of heaven as we keep our eyes upon Him through each day.

RESPECTING THE HOLY SPIRIT

Holy Father, bless Your holy name! Your majesty and holiness exceed our ability to understand. We are shielded from beholding Your fullness, for our sinful frame would be consumed in the brightness of Your glory. It is Your grace that is gentle with us, as well as patient and longsuffering. At times, we treat You with too much familiarity, and by doing so we, in ignorance, show a lack of respect. Through grace we are forgiven and made comfortable in Your presence, but do not let that comfort lead to any less sanctity in our relationship with You. Thou art the Almighty! May we humble ourselves in Your presence and not forget from where we have come... even death in our sins. Thank You for life and cleansing through Jesus, in whose name we pray. Amen.

UZZAH PUT FORTH HIS HAND TO THE ARK OF GOD (II SAM. 6:6)

Our God is holier than we know! His glory exceeds what we are able to comprehend while yet in this body of flesh. Even Paul explained that we "see through a glass darkly," but that the day was coming when we would "know, even as we are known." (See I Cor. 13:12.) Even as God hid Himself in a cloud when communicating with the children of Israel following their exodus from Egypt, so we are somewhat shielded from the fullness of His glory even today. Those who have seen Him clearer have been moved to fall upon their faces in His presence. John, a disciple who walked with

Jesus, when seeing Him in the reality of the Spirit said, in Revelations 1: 17, "And when I saw him, I fell at his feet as dead." John had spent much time with Jesus and was very close to Him as a disciple. Yet, when seeing His majesty and power in the Spirit, he fell on his face. This is the supreme act of submission and humility. John, by doing so, was acknowledging the deity of Jesus. Although Jesus had called His disciples "friends," John was seeing much more than a friend: He was seeing His God.

Sometimes, as we become more conversant with the things of God - His Word, prayer, worship, and the activities that accompany the Christian faith - we can slip into behavior that is less than proper. Things can creep into our attitudes and actions that are not glorifying to the Lord. The respect and awe that should cause us to humble ourselves can be missing, or lost, if we touch the things of God with too much familiarity and too little respect and holy fear. This can lead to the flavor and leaven of the world polluting our testimony and lifestyle. If we are careless with the things that are holy, we stand on dangerous ground in the Spirit, though we are under grace. Deception, error, and sin await us if we step into the wrong heart attitude concerning God and the spiritual things of ministry. To touch the things of God today, in Christian service and witness, is to touch the same holiness kept in the Ark of God in Old Testament times. He is the same God yesterday, today and *forever*. While we are under grace and not under the law, still we are wise to guard our hearts against any attitude that would tarnish the ways of the Spirit or cast a worldly or lower nature hue upon the things of God.

Uzzah fell into this trap of being too familiar with the holiness of God. During the wars of Israel, the ark of God had been captured, and then returned and found itself in the house of Abinadab. David, once secure upon the throne as king, desired to bring the ark to Jerusalem. This became a great event. David took with him thirty thousand men, and with all the people went to bring the ark from the house of Abinadab. The ark was placed upon a wooden cart that was pulled by oxen. The two sons of Abinadab, Ahio and Uzzah, led the cart. God had given extremely specific instructions concerning the ark: who could carry it and how it was to be handled. The ark was to be carried by the Levites on their shoulders using the staves God had instructed to be made for that purpose. (See Numbers, 4:5-6.) It was not to be carried on a cart, which was how the Philistines returned the ark to Israel (I Sam. 6:7). Further, the ark was not to be touched by even the Levites, under the penalty of death (Numbers 4: 15). Perhaps we would judge this a small detail, but God demands that we respect His instructions and thus show respect for Him. As they traveled, the movement of the oxen shook the cart as they approached Nachon's threshing floor. Uzzah put forth his hand to prevent the ark from falling. This angered God, for in treating the ark with unholy familiarity, Uzzah had crossed the line and disobeyed the Word of God. This transgression cost Uzzah his life (II Sam. 6:7).

Perhaps Uzzah became too comfortable with the ark while it remained in his father's house. The holiness of the ark had not changed, nor had God's instructed attitude toward it, but Uzzah's attitude was disrespectful. Handling the ark in the same fashion that the non-believing Philistines had done was the first mistake (the cart pulled by oxen). The ways of the world had affected the way Israel was approaching God. Later, in I Chronicles 15, we read of David returning to properly bring the ark to Jerusalem. In verse two he says, "none ought to carry the ark of God but the Levites." In verse 13 David acknowledges the prior error saying, "For because ye did it not at the first, the Lord our God made a breach upon us, for that we sought him not after the due order."

This story demonstrates the dangers of allowing an attitude to develop which is too casual in its approach to God. Such an attitude demeans the holiness of the Lord and grieves the Holy Spirit. It finds as its source the darkness of the world around us and the hateful influence of Satan: the one who shows no respect for God and His authority. A good measure of holy fear is healthy in our handling the things of God. Without it we could easily be found to place the glories of the Spirit on a wooden cart behind oxen; a place God never intended them to be. The ark was to be carried by wooden staves placed through four golden rings attached to the ark. We too must learn to handle the things of the Spirit with the "wood" of humility and the "gold" of holiness. Any influence from the flesh or the world must be rejected, for the things of the Spirit are not to be handled with such things.

LIFE'S RESTRICTIONS ...
HOW THEY BLESS US

Heavenly Father, Shepherd of our souls, forgive us for our impetuous ways and impatient hearts. Forgive us for our lack of faith, which we have often displayed through our questioning of the way You have placed before us. We acknowledge You in all things. In the common moments, yes in every moment, we acknowledge You as the Lord of that moment. You know precisely the purpose of every detail of our lives. Everything around us, we place upon the altar and give it unto You. We do not wish to escape it, but rather to learn from it the gem of light You wish to give. Though we may struggle to understand, we trust You, and know that the precious Holy Spirit will help us to yield, for our desire is to fulfill Your will. Thank You for the Teacher, who is able to enlighten our hearts. In Jesus's name we pray. Amen.

WHATSOEVER TOUCHETH THE ALTAR
SHALL BE HOLY (EXODUS 29:37)

The Lord takes the things most common and transforms them into things most holy. Common sheep and livestock, dwelling in the fields and fences of God's people, became holy offerings unto God when placed upon the altar of sacrifice. The altar sanctified the gift (Matt.23:19). The gift of itself was not a holy thing. The one thing that separated one sheep from another, to make it holy, was not the beauty of the pasture in which it dwelt, nor the cleanliness of its wool, but the altar upon which it was offered. The altar of sacrifice made the offering holy and acceptable to God. The correct altar made the common into something holy.

There is an altar of sacrifice today that serves the same purpose. It is in the temple of the Lord, just as the altar of old. However, the temple has changed. The temple of God is now the heart of the believer. Scripture teaches us that we are the temple of the Holy Spirit (I Cor. 6:19). Therefore, all that we offer upon the altar of our hearts becomes holy unto the Lord. Further, all that touches our life, which we offer unto the Lord, becomes something that God uses to further His purposes in our growth and walk with Him. In fact, there is nothing that touches our life that does not become an instrument in the Master's loving hand, to be used for our edification and benefit, when offered to Him in an attitude of willing sacrifice. It is when we struggle against the instruments He chooses that we create more pain for ourselves and hinder His loving work. As we willingly place all things upon the altar of total yielding, we discover more quickly the lesson to be learned.

God uses every circumstance in our lives to discipline our souls and enlighten our minds to understand His ways. The pressures, restrictions, responsibilities, and adversities are necessary for our growth. The Lord takes the valleys of our lives when it is difficult to continue, the mountainous terrain that seems impassable, the crooked paths where we cannot see, and the rough places that seem too challenging, and through them reveals His glory to us (Isaiah 40: 1-5). It is when we question them that we delay the process of spiritual development. Every common thing that touches our lives, when offered upon the altar of our heart, is swiftly transformed into an instrument of light that opens our eyes to better understand the Lord. God is in the limits and restrictions of our lives, and it is when we acknowledge Him in all things that we find enlightenment. It is faith that enables us to acknowledge Him in everything that touches our lives. It requires this faith to please Him. This inner action is quite different from the impostor of religious activity.

In John 10, Jesus speaks of being the door to the sheep. He speaks also of others trying to climb in without coming through the Door. The picture we see is one of an enclosed area with a door and fences or walls. This must be the case, for if He were speaking only of open pastures, there would be no door, nor anything to climb over. The picture portrays some restrictions placed upon His sheep. They were behind the door, and inside the fences. It is inside the restrictions of life that we learn to hear His voice and understand His ways. Responsibilities, difficulties, requirements, limitations which are in our lives are God's fences, boundaries set to protect and prepare us. It is the impostor that romps, undisciplined, in the pastures outside the sheepfold of the Spirit to encourage us to escape from God's fences. It was the impostor that attempted to climb into the sheepfold, bypassing the Door, to get at the sheep (John 10:1). When Jesus did lead the sheep out of the fold, they had become familiar with His voice. Because of this, they could stay close to Him in the freedom of the open pastures (John 10:3-5). The discipline learned inside the limits of the fold prepares the soul for a spiritual walk when the limits are relaxed or removed.

If we understand the way of the Spirit, we then know that the perceived limitations and the responsibilities of life are the fences of God's love that protect us until we have become so yielded to Him that, even without fences, we will walk only in the steps of our Shepherd and not dare go astray. Those who listen to the impostor, jump the fences, into seemingly glorious freedom, premature to learning the deeper disciplines of the Lord. The pastures are full of religious impostors that cannot lead the sheep to the deeper truths of the Spirit. It is the impostor that attempts to tell us the fences and disciplines of God's sheepfold are not spiritual and should be ignored. The truth is, that the true freedom and revelation of the Holy Spirit come to us as we accept the apparent limitations and restrictions.

It is by yielding to them, not avoiding or resisting them, that we find our eyes opened and our hearts filled with His presence. It is when we place the fences around our lives upon the altar of our heart that our spirit is freed from selfishness and sin. Leaping with the impostor through the fields of religious works is not the way of the Spirit. We must learn the disciplines of God's fences to grow in the Spirit. They are for our protection and blessing.

Faith and trust in God allow us to live day by day, knowing that our steps are ordered by the Lord. We do not need to question the path. We do not need to figure out a better way. We can trust in His wisdom and yield to the order of the day, for it is His order. We can rest in the fold and not press against the fences, for our Shepherd has placed us here for our benefit. We must learn to hear His voice and distinguish it from the imposter before we dare venture into the open pastures. There are dangers in the outer pastures for which He is preparing us, as we are willing to rest in the fold of His choosing. It is inside the fold that our will is sacrificed and His is learned. When His will has become ours, we will no longer see any fences, nor valleys, nor mountains, nor rough or crooked places, but only our Shepherd.

GOD HEARS YOUR PRAYERS

Heavenly Father, forgive us for our misunderstanding as it relates to the wonders of Your grace. We rejoice to know that through faith we are saved and justified in Your eyes, not by our own works. Keep us from the bondage of thinking that our own efforts improve us in Your sight. Let us forever stay focused upon the glorious sacrifice of Jesus and the greatness and perfection of His name. We are awed by the power of the name in which we pray: the name of Jesus. Amen.

AND HIS NAME, THROUGH FAITH IN HIS NAME (ACTS 3:16)

What can I add to my prayers to make them more effective? In the Old Testament of the Bible, man was required to bring sacrifices and offerings to God. Some of these were sin offerings, while others were to demonstrate thankfulness. Are there offerings or sacrifices that I can bring today to improve my chances of getting an answer to my prayers? This question has a strange ring... and it should. Such thinking rings of works rather than faith. "What can I do?" "What can I add?" "What can I bring to get more of God's attention and response?" These are questions that lead toward our own effort in attempting to become better in God's eyes. The initial question of, "how can my prayers become more effective," is a good question. Where we take our search for the answer is a possible area of concern. We may choose from many paths in our walk with God. It is possible to take a wrong turn. Sound teaching in the things of the Spirit will help us to make the correct choice. These are not necessarily paths in the physical world, but in the world of thought and spirit. Mind sets develop which, if we are not careful, can sidetrack us in the realm of the spirit.

Thinking which takes us away from the simplicity and power of faith is destructive. It is grieving to the work of the Holy Spirit and brings bondage to our souls. Paul watched with great concern as the Galatians were swept up with a similar mind set. They were attempting to add works to the foundation of faith in Jesus. They were "thinking" that by doing certain things they would become more acceptable to God. They yielded to the wrong concept: adding the works of the law to their faith in Jesus. Paul called this thinking a perversion of the Gospel of Christ. (See Gal. 1: 7.) Any such thinking is opposite to the teachings of Jesus, the receiving of salvation, and the indwelling of the Holy Spirit. Paul asked the Galatians in chapter 3, verses 2-3, "This only would I learn of you, received ye the Spirit by the works of the law, or by the hearing of faith? Are ye so foolish? Having begun in the Spirit, are ye now made perfect by the flesh?" He previously stated to them, "even we have believed in Jesus Christ, that we might be justified by the faith of Christ, and not by the works of the law: for by the works of the law shall no flesh be justified" (Gal. 2:16). "For in Jesus Christ neither circumcision availeth anything, nor uncircumcision; but faith which worketh by love" (Gal. 5:6). Thinking which makes me perform, in order to receive favor from God, takes me out of God's grace and places me under a form of religious law. This is a realm in which faith is inoperative. In Gal 5:4, Paul says that if I place the burden of righteousness upon myself, and think to accomplish it by my works, then I have fallen from grace.

The same principle holds true concerning my prayers. I cannot add anything to them to make them more effective. If I bind myself with a vow to display to God how serious I am about my request, it does not add effectiveness to my prayers. If I pledge to do acts of goodness continually, or to not do certain things that displease Him ever again, even then I add nothing to the power of my prayers. The secret of effective praying is faith and obedience: faith in His name and faith in His sacrifice. When Jesus was asked, "what must man do to work the works of God," He said, "This is the work of God, that ye believe on him whom he hath sent" (John 6:28-29). Jesus tells us to pray in His name. "And whatsoever ye shall ask in my name, that will I do, that the Father may be glorified in the Son." (See John 14:13; 15:16.) A foundational truth to effective prayer is not only faith, but obedience to God. John 15:7 says, "If ye abide in me, and my words abide in you, ye shall ask what ye will, and it shall be done unto you." The "if" is up to us. If we yield our hearts to obey, then our prayers hold great power. Without this foundation, we cannot expect God to answer our prayers. We may be praying for many things, and He will bring us back to the point of obedience, which point may not be anywhere near the subject matter of our unyielded prayers. Seeking to hear His voice, and be obedient to His whispers in our hearts is the way to more effective prayer. If the heavens seem like brass in our prayer life, then we need to seek to find where we may have been disobedient to God in some way.

When we come to God in prayer, we need to come holding up the name of Jesus. There is no more powerful way to pray. When we come in His name, we come with full access to God. God the Father gives us His full attention when we come in His Son's name. How much faith we place in His name is the key. Good works do not add any power to the name of Jesus. Acts of sacrifice do not make His name more effective with the Father. We cannot add to His name, nor to His sacrifice. Jesus's shed blood is the complete and perfect sacrifice which opens fully heaven's doors, and God's heart, to the believer. It is a mistake to think we need to add acts of duty or sacrifice to each prayer to get them through to God. We would soon be needing a logbook to keep track of everything we promised God.

Such a stance is folly and not of faith. If we think to add our works to what Jesus has already accomplished, then, in our own hearts, we cheapen His sacrifice and weaken His name. Ponder this for a moment: what could we add to the holy blood of Christ to make us more acceptable to God? Shall we add a week of fasting? Shall we add a large sum of money to tithe? Shall we pledge to do good deeds daily for the rest of our life? Clearly, the answer to each of these is, nothing can add to the precious work of Jesus in offering Himself as the sacrifice for our sins. And, as we think about His name, what could we possibly add to make the name of Jesus more acceptable to the Father. Foolish thinking isn't it.

Therefore, when we pray, let us take hold of His name wholeheartedly! Let us place our utmost confidence in the fact that when we come to prayer in His name, we are heard! He has promised! It is holy fact that God will listen, regardless of our flaws and lack of perfection. To place faith in anything other than His name is sin. How dare we think that even the best of our own efforts could ever add anything to His wonderful and glorious name. When the lame man was healed in Acts 3, Peter explained, "Ye men of Israel, why marvel ye at this? or why look ye so earnestly on us, as though by our own power or holiness we had made this man to walk?... His name, through faith in His name hath made this man strong whom ye see and know: yea, the faith which is by Him hath given him this perfect soundness in the presence of you all" (Acts 3: 12 & 16). Praise God! He has given us the ultimate and complete key to effective prayer: the blood of Jesus to cleanse us and make us accepted of God, and the Name of Jesus to use when we approach His holy throne. Faith and obedience are the only ingredients to be added. (See Hebrews 11:6.)

THE EXCELLENT WAY OF LOVE

Heavenly Father, with each passing day You impress us yet more with Your love and concern for our souls. You look past our misunderstandings and encourage us with Your wisdom and instruction. You are a gentle husbandman who works carefully in the garden of our hearts. You prune the dead and non-productive branches to encourage a more fruitful expression. The motive of Your work is love, and for this we thank You and praise You. This love was embodied in the coming of Jesus to this earth. This was the great love of God that Jesus should lay down His life for sinful man. Thank You Lord. We are grateful for our salvation. In Jesus's name we pray. Amen.

A MORE EXCELLENT WAY (I COR. 12:31)

Love! God's love for man moved Him to send Jesus as the sacrifice for sin. As certain shepherds stood in the field the night Jesus was born, they were greeted by an angel. The message from this angel was, "behold, I bring you good tidings of great joy, which shall be to all people. For unto you is born this day in the city of David a Savior, which is Christ the Lord" (Luke 2:10). This was a tremendous message of "great joy." How excited this angel must have been to be able to announce Jesus's birth. Other heavenly beings were standing by listening to the announcement. Once the angel had made his proclamation, they could no longer be silent. The news was too exciting! They had to join in, as we read in verse 13, "And suddenly there was with the angel a multitude of the heavenly host praising God, and saying, Glory to God in the highest, and on earth peace, good will toward men."

How stunned these shepherds must have been. They were taken up in the moment, as a multitude of spiritual beings were proclaiming glory to God and good will toward men. They heard firsthand the wondrous news of the Saviors' birth, as they were lifted from the pastures in which they stood into the presence of God's glory. Heaven was excited on this day when Jesus was born. The announcement reflected their great joy and enthusiasm over what had occurred. This was a very big occasion. The Lamb of God had been born. Not merely another sacrifice upon the altar under the law, but the final sacrifice for man's sin. Jesus was the one who would pay the final and complete price to redeem man to God. All the sacrifices under the law could not add up to pay for this purchase. They fell short in the books of heaven. The blood of bulls and goats was not valuable enough to pay for the soul of man. It would take the blood of the Lamb of God, Jesus! (Hebrews 9:13-14; 25-28; 10:1.)

The law did well in defining sin. As Paul said, "I had not known sin, but by the law: for I had not known lust, except the law had said, thou shalt not covet" (Romans 7:7; also see Romans 7:13). The problem lay in the fact that the law was spiritual, and man was carnal. Man could not attain unto the righteousness required by the law. Man kept falling short. Thus, man kept offering sacrifices for his sin, repeatedly. The problem of sin in man was an inner problem, deep within the heart. The law could not reach this area with any transforming power. This problem could only be fixed by an indwelling of holiness. The Spirit of God would have to enter the heart of man to fix the problem from the inside out. The law only addressed the outer issue of showing sin to be sin, and of offering the shedding of blood to cover the act of sin. It did not strike at the root of sin. It did not transform the sinner into a new creature.

God knew of the problem. His love desired man to be free from sin on the inside. So, we read of God's gift to man in Romans 8:3-4. "For what the law could not do, in that it was weak through the flesh, God sending his own Son in the likeness of sinful flesh, and for sin, condemned sin in the flesh: that the righteousness of the law might be fulfilled in us, who walk not after the flesh, but after the Spirit." God said, "I will fix the problem. I will cleanse man from all of his sin with the blood of my Son. I will make him holy in My sight, so that I might indwell him with My Spirit. I will give man the power to overcome from within."

The "New Covenant" in Jesus's blood was designed to write God's laws within our heart. This was the inward solution to the problem. From within our own hearts, we were to see, know, and be empowered, to live up to the righteousness of God. This was made possible because of His presence within us, not because of our own power or goodness. Hebrews 8:10 reads, "For this is the covenant that I will make with the house of Israel after those days, saith the Lord; I will put my laws into their mind and write them in their hearts: and I will be to them a God, and they shall be to me a people." It is no wonder the angel and the hosts of heaven were excited to announce the birth of Jesus. A glorious mystery was unfolding before their eyes.

Goodwill toward man was the message from the hosts of heaven; God's love reaching out to us while we were yet in sin. This is the motive of all that God desires to accomplish in our hearts and lives as Christians. God loves us when He chastens us and seeks to bring us into a place of greater blessing and righteousness. God loves us when we are struggling and does not condemn us for our yet untransformed imperfections. God loves us when we fall and seek recovery. God wants those who reject Him to receive His love, if only they will ask. God cares deeply for all mankind, for it was to all men that the good tidings were heralded.

Paul, in chapter 13 of I Corinthians, speaks of the more excellent way of love, or charity. Not to oversimplify, but it could be written in one word.

Jesus! For all of the attributes of love, as described in this chapter, are found in the life and expression of Jesus while He was on the earth. He had all power, knowledge, and wisdom, yet came with overflowing compassion and concern to touch the battered and suffering lives of many. He forgave the adulteress who others sought to condemn. He was the fullness of the good tidings and great joy over which all of heaven rejoiced. He is the more excellent way! May His Spirit and love find more expression through us, and may our hearts and minds be kept in the way that is truly more excellent - the way of God's love.

WHAT BASICS DID JESUS AND THE EARLY CHURCH LAY AS PART OF THE FOUNDATION OF CHRISTIAN FAITH AND FELLOWSHIP?

There is significant importance in understanding the "basics" of the Christian faith, to properly solidify a good foundation in our faith. Today, Christianity has become a faith of "many flavors." It is like Baskins- Robins 31 flavors of ice cream. Pick the one you want, the one that tastes best to you. If you do not like the ingredients in one flavor, walnuts, or almonds, then choose another.

But what if some flavors are not good for you? What if some hinder the full development in Christ. What if some are harmful to obtaining a better understanding of God? What if some violate the intentions of Scripture? What if some leave out extremely healthy ingredients necessary for us?

Paul, in Galatians 1, speaks clearly that the Gospel that he presented should not be modified, diluted, or added to in extremely strong language. "I marvel that you are so soon removed from him that called you into the grace of Christ unto another gospel: which is not another; but there be some that trouble you and would pervert the gospel of Christ. But though we, or an angel from heaven, preach any other gospel unto you than that which we have preached unto you, let him be accursed. As we said before, so say I now again, if any man preaches any other gospel unto you than that ye have received, let him be accursed." He repeats the admonishment twice, "let him be accursed." This adds great emphasis to the statement. Interesting that he says, "which is not another" gospel. In other words, it retained enough of the original gospel message to sound like it was the correct and full gospel. But it was not. It was polluted enough to alarm Paul to warn the hearers.

Paul alludes to the origin of this "polluted gospel" as being for the purpose of pleasing man, or some men at least. For what purpose? To not offend perhaps, or bend to a certain less offensive presentation of Jesus and His shed blood? For we read in Galatians 1:10, "for do I now persuade (pacify, conciliate) men, or God? Or do I seek to please men? For if I yet pleased men, I should not be the servant of Christ." The truth of the Gospel will always offend some! Look at the persecution of the believers and the crucifixion of Jesus!

From this warning, let us look at what the Gospel was, as presented by Paul, Jesus, and the early church leaders in the book of Acts. Let us accept Paul's warning and apply it to what we see from this and adhere to that original simple Gospel. Let us look at the "back to basics" of the Gospel as set in motion by Jesus, and as presented by the early church apostles.

The basics are important. Using football as an analogy for a moment, the basics required before going out on the playing field include a good amount of gear, a helmet, pads, proper shoes etc. If a player were to play without a helmet, or without protective pads, injuries would be severe and potential deadly. Taking a hard hit to the unprotected head by another player's helmet would be disastrous. The "basics" are especially important to be properly equipped to resist the works of the devil, develop into a mature powerful believer, and sustain a close walk with Jesus.

Basics phase I

What is the Gospel that should be presented in fellowships today?

The Gospel overview is this: God the Father, sent His Son Jesus, into the world to redeem mankind from their sins, and to fulfill the Old Testament prophecies given to the Jewish prophets of old. As Paul explains in Ephesians 2, Jesus fulfilled the promises made to Israel of old, extended God's promise of salvation to the non-Jewish world, the gentiles, and made both the chosen Jewish people and the gentiles one in Him through the shedding of His blood sacrifice. The Holy spirit remains with us today, after Jesus's death and resurrection, as our comforter, our teacher, our guide, and the power of God dwelling within the believer. God is the mystery of the "three in one," the Father, the Son, and the Holy Spirit.

Jesus, God's only begotten Son, died for our sins, rose again from the dead, and it is His shed blood which cleanses our sins, if we ask for forgiveness and believe. It requires a person to repent, to change their thinking, to seek forgiveness for their sins. Below are just a few of the scriptures related to this foundational truth.

I Corinthians, 2:2: Paul states here, "For I determined to know anything among you, save Jesus Christ, and him crucified."

Acts 20:28: "The church of God, which He purchased with His own blood."

John 3:16: "For God so loved the world, that He gave His only begotten Son, that whoever believe in Him should not perish but have everlasting life."

Romans 3:25: "Whom God hath set forth to be a propitiation through faith in his blood, to declare his righteousness for the remission of sins that are past..."

Hebrews 9:22 "and without the shedding of blood there is no remission."

I Corinthians 15:3-4; "For I delivered unto you first of all that which I also received, how that Christ died for our sins according to the scriptures; and that he was buried, and that he rose again the third day according to the scriptures."

Acts 3:19: "Repent ye therefore, and be converted, that your sins may be blotted out."

Luke: 24:47: "and that repentance and remission of sins should be preached in his name among all nations."

John adds the following in I John 1:9: "if we confess our sins, he is faithful and just to forgive us our sins, and to cleanse us from all unrighteousness." And in 1:7, ".and the blood of Jesus Christ his Son cleanses us from all sin."

The presentation of the Gospel should include these basics: that it is the sacrifice of Jesus on the Cross, His crucifixion, shedding of His cleansing blood, and resurrection from the dead that saves us as we believe. If the blood of Jesus is not presented, then in what do we trust for the washing of our sins? A "Gospel" which is bloodless is also void of salvation! Offensive? Sure, to the ignorant or rebellious. Necessary to present? Absolutely! Paul says he will not be ashamed of the Gospel of Christ, nor of His shed blood, nor of His resurrection and promise of eternal life. (Romans 1:16) Neither should we. It is the heart and spirit of a lost soul that will resonate with the truth of the Gospel (the pure, "offensive," uncompromised truth of death, spilling of His blood, and resurrection). As offensive as it is to the natural pride and carnal understanding, it is the only message that will save a soul through faith. To appeal to the mental capacity of the lost through a diluted gospel, misses the target and can misrepresent the truth of salvation. Take Jesus's blood from the message and you earn Paul's admonition of being accursed.

Basics Phase II

What importance did the Church fathers place upon the Baptism of the Holy Spirit?

What importance did Jesus place upon the Baptism of the Holy Spirit?

What did Jesus instruct his disciples after he rose from the dead? And think on this for one moment, were they born again and saved at this point? They had learned of Him during His ministry with them. They knew He was the Messiah. They had seen Him die. They had seen Him Resurrected. Thomas crying out "my Lord and my God." Jesus was seen of them forty days after His resurrection, sharing with them the things of the kingdom of God. I believe they were certainly born again when Jesus said the following things to them.

Mark 16:15-18, Jesus says to them, "Go ye into all the world, and preach the gospel to every creature. He that believes and is baptized shall be saved; but he that believes not shall be damned. And these signs shall follow them that believe; in my name shall they cast out devils; they shall speak with new tongues; they shall take up serpents; and if they drink any deadly thing, it shall not hurt them; they shall lay hands on the sick and they shall recover."

Acts: 1:3-8 selected passages: "… to whom also he shewed himself alive after his passion by many infallible proofs, being seen of them forty days, and speaking of the things pertaining to the kingdom of God: and being assembled together with them, commanded them that they should not depart from Jerusalem, but wait for the promise of the Father, which saith he, ye have heard of me. For John truly baptized with water; but you shall be baptized with the Holy Spirit not many days hence….ye shall receive power, after that the Holy Spirit is come upon you; and ye shall be witnesses unto me…unto the uttermost part of the earth."

Jesus had commanded them to go into all the world and preach the Gospel to every creature, but here He clarifies, "but not just yet." You first need to be baptized with the Holy Spirit. They needed the power of the Holy Spirit. They needed the gifting of the Holy Spirit. Jesus commanded them to wait for it. It was not a request, but a command.

Did the apostles carry this priority, being baptized by the Holy Spirit, into their ministry after Jesus ascended into heaven?

Let us look at a few cases presented in the book of Acts. In Acts 2, the disciples received the baptism of the Holy Spirit themselves, and Jesus words were fulfilled. They received the Holy Spirit as He said they would, and they also spoke with other tongues as the Spirit gave them utterance, as Jesus had said.

In Acts 8, Phillip was evangelizing in Samaria, and people were saved, devils were being cast out, and healings were occurring. Again, a fulfillment of Jesus's words. When the disciples heard about this, they immediately sent Peter and John "who...prayed for them that they might receive the Holy Spirit." Acts 8:15. Basically they said, "alright guys, there are a bunch of new believers over there in Samaria, Peter, John, you go over there and make sure they receive the Holy Spirit." For that is the first thing we read they did upon arriving there.

In Acts 10:44-46 we read of the first recorded Gentiles receiving salvation and the baptism of the Holy Spirit. Peter is sharing with them the story of Jesus, his death and resurrection, and the remission of sins through believing in Him when this occurred: "while Peter yet spoke these words, the Holy Spirit fell on all them which heard the word. And they of the circumcision which believed were astonished, as many as came with Peter, because that on the Gentiles also was poured out the gift of the Holy Ghost. For they heard them speak with tongues and magnify God." Here, the Holy Spirit Himself poured out, bearing witness with the words of Peter, and fulfilling the words of Jesus.

In Acts 19, Paul carried the importance of the Holy Spirit baptism in his work as well. As we read in verses 2-6 selected sections: "and he said unto them, have ye received the Holy Spirit since ye believed? ..... and when Paul had laid his hands upon them, the Holy Spirit came on them; and they spoke with tongues and prophesied."

The manifestations of the Holy Spirit, and His gifts intended to operate in and through the believer, are important basics to the faith. In Corinthians, Paul addresses this subject in detail. Criticizing the out of order use of the gifts, while encouraging them when done decently and in order. He addresses the personal edification one receives from praying in the spirit (in tongues) in I Corinthians 14:4 saying, "he that speaks in an unknown tongue edifies himself."

He sets the priority for church gatherings as being that of edifying others, not simply everyone speaking in tongues. Paul explains in I Corinthians 14:22-25, that if in church gatherings there is no order to the gifts, and there is a display of chaos with everyone babbling in tongues, visitors would think the Christians were out of their minds. Paul continues to explain that if in church gatherings someone speaks forth an inspired word from the Lord, so people can understand what is being said, this would result in non-believers turning to the Lord because God spoke to their hearts and revealed things to them in the spirit. This reaction would likely have been to an inspired word that the Holy Spirit knew was needed for one or more persons, or perhaps a word of knowledge revealing a specific thing known only to the heart of the person or persons the inspired word was for.

Paul then goes on to say that when they gather for fellowship, there can be a speaking in tongues, if there is also an interpretation of what was said. And then Paul lays out an orderly church service, including the gifts of the Spirit. And concludes in verse 39-40, "wherefore, brethren, covet to prophesy, and forbid not to speak with tongues. Let all things be done decently and in order."

From a personal growth and edification point of view, Paul further explains in I Corinthians 14:14-19 selected passages: "if I pray in an unknown tongue, my spirit prays, but my understanding is unfruitful. What is it then? I will pray with the spirit, and I will pray with the understanding also: I will sing with the spirit, and I will sing with the understanding also....I thank my God, I speak with tongues more than ye all: yet in the church I had rather speak five words with my understanding, that by my voice I might teach others also, than ten thousand words in an unknown tongue."

My personal observation of Paul boasting that he spoke in tongues more than everyone else is this: it would be rather nasty of spirit for him to say this if the prayer language of the Spirit was only for some believers and not available for all. In every case in scripture where there was the Baptism of the Holy Spirit, they spoke with tongues, as foretold by Jesus (with one exception noted below). As a side note, Jesus did not say that "some of those who believe will speak with other tongues," He said, "those that believe." In I Corinthians 12, Paul asks, "Are all apostles? Are all prophets? Are all teachers? Are all workers of miracles? Do all have gifts of healings? Do all speak with tongues? Do all interpret?" It is my belief that this scripture section was discussing the gifts of the Spirit in relation to ministering to others and to the church when assembled together. I think that the prayer language of the spirit, to pray in tongues, is something available to every believer as a blessing in prayer and for edification. This statement is in no way a judgement upon those who do not use this prayer gift, nor a mandate that they must. It is an encouragement that it is available to all who ask and believe, and that you can.

In summary, Scripture outlines several different uses and benefits of speaking in tongues. There is the private use for prayer and edification. There is the public use to be accompanied with an interpretation so all can be edified. And there is singing in the Spirit. Personally, I believe that all these things can be done in times of fellowship if they are done decently and in order. Often in times of worship many will sing in the spirit, in a way that flows with the overall worship and is not disruptive. Or some will quietly pray in the spirit when there is a time of prayer. I believe this is very acceptable, and should be encouraged. I think that Paul's summary statement is a great guideline, "wherefore, brethren, covet to prophesy, and forbid not to speak with tongues. Let all things be done decently and in order."

Taking this to the actual operation of this gift of prayer in the Spirit and putting it into practice, we should understand that when we worship in our native tongue (English, Spanish etc.) we exhale, make a vocal noise and fashion our words. When learning a new foreign language, it is the same, we must try to say a word, which may not sound very close to the actual dialect when we first start. When I first tried to speak Spanish words, they sounded more like garble than Spanish! It is the same with the spiritual language. We must loosen ourselves to make a vocal noise, allow sounds to come forth, move our tongues and allow the syllables to be fashioned without thought of how it sounds. Our attention should be on worshiping the Lord, not focused on how silly it sounds. If you think about it, to our human intelligence, it is very stupid and ridiculous to speak in this fashion. In God's eyes, I think it is more like we are humbled, releasing our control over this expression to the Holy Spirit, laying aside our human intellect and not attempting to understand this gift and how it edifies. But it does edify!

The one time that the comment about the baptism of the Holy Spirit does not specifically state that they spoke with tongues was in Act 8:14-18. However, it says that Simon, when he "saw that through the laying on of the apostles hands the Holy Spirit was given, he offered them money..." wanting the same ability to do this. What did Simon observe when the Holy Spirit was given through the laying on of hands that prompted this comment? Simon must have seen or heard something. Based on every other account of the Baptism of the Holy Spirit, and the words of Jesus, I think Simon saw what the Jewish believers saw when Cornelius and his family and friends received the Holy Spirit baptism, "And they of the circumcision which believed were astonished, as many as came with Peter, because that on the Gentiles also was poured out the gift of the Holy Spirit. For they heard them speak with tongues and magnify God." They knew because they heard them speak with tongues and magnify God.

There are many gifts of the Holy Spirit, and many manifestations. The speaking in tongues can be in prayer, in song, or in a speaking forth with interpretation. Not everyone speaks forth in a tongue in a gathering with interpretation, but I do believe that all can pray and sing in the spirit personally, as Paul stated...he did that more than anyone else. Why? It edified him, built him up, and comforted him. Something every believer is entitled to. And when orderly, I personally believe that providing an opportunity for worship in song in the spirit is appropriate, as is the quiet praying in the spirit at times when gathered together, as long as this does not disrupt the gathering.

If we employ Paul's admonition about love, in I Corinthians 13, and combine that with the gifts of the Holy Spirit, we will be safe, and God will be glorified. Prophecy shall one day cease, as will tongues, knowledge will vanish, but love will remain. Though we operate in all of the gifts of tongues, prophecy, knowledge, faith to move mountains, yet do not operate with love as our source and foundation, we are nothing! We are out of God's order in the spirit. The gifts of the Holy Spirit will always flow in love because God is love. Paul presents chapter 13 as the prelude to spiritual gifts. It can be viewed as the foundation for their operation. Following his admonition to seek Charity first, he then says, "Follow after charity, and desire spiritual gifts." I Corinthians 14:1.

In summary, the basic gospel message, as presented by Jesus and the disciples after His ascension, to fully equip the believer included:

Jesus, the only begotten Son of God dying for our sins, shedding his blood to cleanse our sins, rising from the dead to demonstrate His promise to the believer of eternal life. Repentance is required to receive remission of sins. A person must confess their sins to God, and then He is faithful to forgive and cleanse them of all sin. And the baptism of the Holy Spirit. And as presented, it was most often a second event following salvation, and was treated by the apostles as a priority for believers, based on the records shared with us in the book of Acts.

Stick to the basics! They are important.

SOMETIMES THE OPPOSITION IS ALL SMOKE

Heavenly Father, encourage our hearts in the face of challenge and opposition. Let us not be overly distracted by the enemy's attacks, because we know he is an already defeated foe. May we keep our hands busy with the task at hand and our eyes upon You. Remind us always of Your faithfulness, power, and victory. Grant that we may be useful in accomplishing all of Your desires and purposes on earth. Fill us with Your confidence and determination. In Jesus's name we pray. Amen.

ARE WE ON THE WRONG PATH WHEN WE FACE INCREASED OPPOSITION?

At times we come through places on our journey where there seems to be an ever-increasing amount of opposition. Things seem to come against us in waves, never ceasing. Each new trial seems to increase in intensity, as the building of a terrible storm. We put our hands to the task at hand, seeking to fulfill the will of God in each day, yet with the mounting opposition and difficulty we easily doubt that we are in the will of God at all. How can it be that we are walking down the correct path when there seems to be such a strong headwind? We would like to walk with the wind at our back, not opposing us. "Where is God in all of the pressure, stress and challenge?" we ask.

More than likely He is right there, in the pressure, in the stress, in the challenge. As Christians, we are on the potter's wheel. We are being shaped and molded. We are being changed by the work of the Holy Spirit within. We are being transformed into the likeness of Jesus. When God saves our souls, we are far from Jesus's likeness. As immature believers, we may pass through times of thinking we are more like Him than we are in reality, somewhat like an eighteen-year old. For some reason, at around that age, a person feels they know everything there is to know. Then, somewhere between twenty-five and fifty (hopefully) we awake to the reality that we are not as smart as we think. So, it is in our spiritual growth. After the honeymoon time of our salvation is over, we are placed on the workbench of God for further transformation.

In the spirit, a Christian is a lot like the city of Jerusalem in the days of Nehemiah. There is a lot of garbage and debris in our hearts that needs to be removed. Our walls of strength and protection are broken and of little use. Our gates (the avenues of access to our heart and mind) are burned and keep little out. In short, we are a mess and need a lot of spiritual construction to become like Jesus. A project which, as Paul alluded to, takes a lifetime (Philippians 3: 12-14).

In the days of Nehemiah, the city of Jerusalem was devastated. The walls were broken down and the gates were burned. The remnant of the Jews living there were in great affliction and reproach (Nehemiah 1:3). God's chosen city, the place of His holy temple, was in ruins. It would require a great effort to restore the city. A great deal of building would need to take place. A huge amount of debris would need to be removed to make a clear foundation for rebuilding. In fact, there was so much to remove that at one point the workers became very discouraged (Nehemiah 4:10).

The book of Nehemiah is a wonderful model of the spiritual walk of the believer. In the beginning of the story, God grants Nehemiah great favor in the eyes of the king, who authorizes him to go to Jerusalem to rebuild the wall and grants him all the materials needed to complete the task (2:5-8). The project starts out easy. The way is opened and made smooth for Nehemiah...in the beginning. This is similar to the honeymoon period we enjoy with the Lord after being saved. Things often seem simply wonderful. However, no sooner has Nehemiah announced his vision to rebuild the wall than opposition arises. Verbal, demeaning opposition comes from Sanballat and Tobiah and others who accuse Nehemiah of plotting to rebel against the king (2:19). With the walls of the city rebuilt, they presume the Jews will be able to defend it successfully, or at least better than in its current state. The repair of the walls represented a surrounding border of protection. The enemy began to fight this at the very beginning, before one stone was repaired.

So, it is with us in the spirit. As God begins to build our inner walls of defense and strength, the enemy will oppose us. As the wall of the city proceeded into the actual construction phase, the adversaries increased their opposition. They spoke with the army, escalated their accusations, and declared that even if they rebuilt the wall, a mere small fox running on it would knock it down (Nehemiah 4:1-3). Sound familiar? The devil often says, "God can't do anything with you, and all of your effort is useless. Give up now. Nothing will ever become of you in the Lord." The enemy hasn't changed his approach in thousands of years. As our walls are built, our understanding of the Word of God and the power of the indwelling Holy Spirit help us to quickly rebuke the lies of the enemy. He has difficulty breaching a strong wall.

When the work on the wall was about halfway completed, the enemy got serious. Sanballat and Tobiah planned a military attack to stop the Jews (Nehemiah 4:7-8). Having received word of the enemy's plan, the workmen prepared themselves, and continued working, each man with his weapon and ready to fight (Nehemiah 4:12-23). As the enemy turns up the opposition, we too need to increase our determination to continue. The Jewish workmen continued to build, and slept in their clothing, with their weapons, ready at any moment for what the enemy would throw at them. We need to be as vigilant, for our adversary roams about looking for someone to destroy. At this same time, there was inner discouragement because of the vast amount of debris that needed to be removed to provide a clean foundation for the repaired wall (Nehemiah 4:10-11). And this came at the time the enemy was planning their attack. We need to guard against such inner discouragement when we find ourselves in the midst of God removing the debris from our hearts. He reveals our flesh nature and its activities, not to discourage us, but to get it out of the way so He can build His beautiful work within us. The devil will turn this into an opportunity to discourage us with his assaults, fiery darts of doubt, resentment, discouragement and a host of others. We need to be smarter than to allow him to succeed.

Next, Nehemiah's enemies moved in close, using diplomacy as a cloak of deception. They were trying to get Nehemiah to lift his head from the work he was doing. They again accused him of plotting to become king and rebelling from king Artaxerxes. They hired and paid people close to Nehemiah to cause him to fear for his life, and act disgracefully. They wrote letters to some in Jerusalem who were loyal to the opposition (Nehemiah 6: 1-14). They even used certain prophets in Jerusalem to oppose the man. The opposition against Nehemiah and the rebuilding of the wall continued to intensify, reaching its peak just before the wall was finished. Was Nehemiah on the correct path? Yes. Did opposition greet him on this path? Yes. Did the opposition increase as Nehemiah proceeded? Yes. Did Nehemiah or the enemy prevail? Nehemiah prevailed. For, when the enemy heard that the wall was completed, we read, "And it came to pass, that when all our enemies heard thereof (that the wall was finished, verse 15) and all the heathen that were about us saw these things, they were much cast down in their own eyes: for they perceived that this work was wrought of our God (Nehemiah 6:16). For all of the threatening of the enemy, not one arrow was shot, not one attack launched, not one threat materialized, and the wall continued to be built, gaining strength with each passing day, until it was completed.

Satan has no power to destroy us or harm us; he can only distract and discourage, and then only if we listen to his lies. Jesus said we have power over the enemy (Luke 10: 19). Just as Nehemiah succeeded in the building of the wall, God will prevail in the building of our spiritual stature in Christ. We too must keep our hands on the work before us, trust in God to accomplish His good work in us, and refuse to listen to the distractions and lies of the enemy. And thank God, when we are made strong, the enemy will be greatly discouraged!

IN TODAY'S WORLD OF TOLERANCE, WHAT IS SIN?

Heavenly Father, we do not like to think of ourselves as sinful, yet all that we do which is not in keeping with Your holiness, Your love, and Your character, is just that, sin. When we fall into selfish actions, angry words, bitter resentment, negative comments about others, and a host of other maladies, we sin against You. Forgive us for our shortcomings. Help us to quickly acknowledge our error and repent. Grant that we might be kept in the ways of the Holy Spirit, and bring glory to Your name, not shame. In Jesus's name we pray. Amen.

WHAT IS SIN? THE NATURE OF SIN AND SINS, TWO SEPARATE ISSUES

To answer this question with great simplicity we could say, "sin is the opposite of everything Jesus is." Jesus was without sin. Scripture tells us that all unrighteousness is sin. Transgressing the law of God is sin. Foolishness is sin. Hate is sin. Knowing what we should do and not doing it is sin (See Proverbs 14:21 & 24:9; James 4:17; I John 3:4 & 5: 17). However, an all-encompassing truth about sin, reaching to its core, is that sin is when we choose, exercise our will, to turn away from God, His Word, His guidance, and His ways. It is when we live in our fallen nature of sin, which originated with Adam, when he, knowing it was in disobedience to God, chose to eat of the tree of knowledge. This fallen nature, or self-nature, thrives when we exercise our power to choose, to the satisfaction of ourselves, in opposition to God. The battle of darkness versus light takes place in the center of our being. Here, we will either continue in the nature of sin, placing our own desires, wants, and plans as the priority, or we will learn to yield to God and become transformed from the old nature of rebellion into the new creature, which is created in His image, the likeness of Jesus. There is then a nature of sin, which all men are born into, and there are sins, which originate from this fallen nature.

Jesus, through the sacrifice of His life on the cross and the atoning blood He shed, takes care of the nature of sin problem, (which, without Him, would condemn us to eternal torment), for all those who receive Him as Savior. It is the Holy Spirit working within us who continues to reduce and eliminate the sins which originate from this fallen nature. We are made welcome by God through faith in His Son, and the Son's atonement on the cross, while the work of the Holy Spirit is in progress. How then do we proceed to discern sin, avoid sinning, and walk in victory? One of the keys is the key of choice. The power to choose, or the power of our will. Deuteronomy 30: 19 says, "I have set before you life and death, blessing and cursing: therefore choose..." There are numerous other admonitions to choose, which is something we must do ourselves; it is not something God does for us. (See Joshua 24:15, I Kings 18:21, Isaiah 7:15-16)

Revelations 3:20 quotes Jesus as saying, "Behold, I stand at the door, and knock: if any man hear my voice, and open the door, I will come into him, and will sup with him, and he with me." Jesus is doing the knocking; we must get up and open the door. Jesus does not say, "Behold, I come to knock your door down." Nor does He say, "Behold, I come to force my way into your heart and life." He knocks at the door of our heart, and waits for us to open. The choice is ours. It is an act of our will.

Once we have received Jesus as Savior, we still must learn to listen for His knock, and open to the Holy Spirit in every moment of our lives. There are many voices knocking to gain our attention. Self-will and demons from hell all stand seeking entrance into the place of decision, action, behavior, thought, and understanding. How can we know which voice is His? We will know by the light of His Word. Adam knew to not eat of the tree of knowledge because God had given him His word on the matter. Having knowledge from the Word, the Bible, is critical to learning to decide how we will live, and to whom we will listen - Satan and his devils, or the Holy Spirit of God. Once we have knowledge, then we must choose to act on it.

In Luke 17: 21, Jesus tells us that the kingdom of God is within us. In Matt. 6:10, Jesus instructs us to pray for the kingdom of God to come, and for God's will to be done. This makes it clear that the working out of God's will is going to take place within our hearts, not only out in the world. We must learn to use the power of our own will to deny the flesh expression. (See Galatians, 5:19-21.) We must choose to rely upon the power of the Holy Spirit within. God's will is worked out in us at home, at the place of our employment, in the common walks of life, the store, the gas station, and every place we go. Our goal is to resemble Jesus, and anywhere our behavior doesn't we need to seek God for help, deny Satan access, and believe God that He will help us as we seek to do His will and learn to delight in pleasing Him. In Matt 12:50, Jesus says that as we do the will of the Father, we are His brothers and sisters. In other words, as we begin to behave like Jesus in daily life, then we demonstrate to the world that we belong to His holy family.

Doing His will cuts to the core of our being, and is often difficult at first, even painful. Self dies slowly, and reluctantly. We tend to offer many excuses of why we cannot do His will. "God wouldn't expect that of me." "But that is not fair." "No one is going to treat me like that." "Who do they think they are?" "Well, I'm not gossiping, but did you hear about thus and such." I'm not speaking evil of anyone, but so and so is sure a troubled person, did you hear what they did?" There can be a time for sharing and discussion but sometimes such reasoning and conversation can be born of sin, and fueled by the enemy, to preserve self and hinder yielding to the will of God. Proverbs 10:19 says, "In the multitude of words there wanteth not sin." In other words, where there is a lot of discussion, one can most likely find sin. We need to watch what we say, and what we think, for we can easily put up a defense around our sinful behavior with much talking about it.

When things got really tough for Jesus, He prayed for the will of the Father to be done. When it was painful to His very core, He yet prayed not for His will, but for the will of the Father (Matt. 26:38-42). Self-protection, self-pride, and all of self's interests were offered to God and yielded to His will. Usually, our attempts to defend ourselves to others is born from our fallen nature. Jesus suffered physical death, public humiliation, looked as though He was a total failure, liar, and fake, as He clung to the will of the Father and He did not defend Himself, but committed Himself to God. Are we prepared to be called His brothers and sisters? It will take the same willingness to be transformed by the Holy Spirit, and die to self. Once we know His purposes, to do anything less is sin.

FINDING GOD'S REST

Heavenly Father, Your promised place of rest for Your people is a place we seek to experience fully. We bring turmoil and difficulty upon ourselves because of our own error and willfulness. Help us to learn to walk with You, heed the loving admonitions of Your great wisdom, and be content as You guide us through life's lessons and blessings. The richness and fullness of joy we find in obedience to You is more precious than words can say. Praise You for Your faithfulness, Your love, Your help, and for the answers to our prayers. In Jesus name we pray. Amen.

REMEMBER THE SABBATH ...TO KEEP IT HOLY (EXODUS 20:8)

The initial Sabbath was God's command for the children of Israel to cease from their labors. He gave them six days to work, but on the seventh they were to not labor (Exodus 20:9-10). On the Sabbath, men stopped their own work and remembered God. The Lord's command was strict and unforgiving. If anyone was found doing their own works on the Sabbath, they were to be put to death. "Ye shall keep the sabbath therefore; for it is holy unto you: everyone that defileth it shall surely be put to death: for whosoever doeth any work therein, that soul shall be cut off from among his people" (Exodus 31:14).

In Numbers chapter 15, a man was found gathering sticks on the Sabbath, probably for cooking or keeping warm. The Lord commanded him to be put to death with stoning. The congregation did so, (verse 36). The breaking of the Sabbath truly meant death.

Keeping the Sabbath meant God's blessing and life. As we read in Isaiah 58:13-14: "If thou turn away thy foot from the Sabbath, from doing thy pleasure on my holy day; and call the Sabbath a delight, the holy of the Lord, honourable; and shalt honour him, not doing thine own ways, nor finding thine own pleasure, nor speaking thine own words; then shalt thou delight thyself in the Lord; and I will cause thee to ride upon the high places of the earth, and feed thee with the heritage of Jacob thy father: for the mouth of the Lord hath spoken it." We are told that the law was our teacher to bring us to Christ (Galatians, 3:24). From it, then, we can learn insight into our current walk with God.

What was the Sabbath? What did it signify and begin to teach God's people? The word Sabbath in Hebrew means "to cease, desist, to intercept, interrupt; implying a complete cessation or a making to cease. The idea is not that of relaxation or refreshment, but cessation from activity." The Sabbath was an interruption in the works and ways of man. A holy intervention saying, "stop from your works and learn of mine, learn to acknowledge Me, your God." How then does this principle apply to us today? We are told in Hebrews 4:9, "There remaineth therefore a rest to the people of God." (This is a Sabbath type rest when we look at the Greek meaning of rest in this verse.) This is not a "doing nothing" rest, but rather a stopping of our own works and efforts, and learning of the ways of the Spirit. Our own works in the flesh are a breaking of the Sabbath rest of God. We will find no peace or blessing in such a state.

Isaiah said it quite completely, as we read in Isaiah 58:13-14, when he said we were to cease from our own ways, stop seeking our own pleasure, and stop speaking our own words. Are we seeking our own will and goals? Do we live to fulfill our own desires and pleasures? What words do we observe coming forth from our lips, for out of the abundance of the heart the mouth speaketh. These are attitudes of the heart which God seeks to transform, so that He may lead us into His rest and peace. Simply put, to enter into God's Sabbath rest, we must cease from our own will. In the areas of our life where we have not yielded self-will to God's control, we will find death, strife, contention, bitterness, and all the works of the flesh. (See Galatians 5:19-21.)

God's principle of death for breaking the Sabbath still has relevance today. In the flesh, we will find spiritual death. Only through obeying in the Spirit will we find blessing and life. The main difference today is that the Sabbath is continual, not only on one day per week. If at any moment we slip into the flesh, we break the spiritual Sabbath of obedience to God's Holy Spirit, and we will find His blessing removed. God interrupted Israel one day a week. The Holy Spirit seeks to continually interrupt us until we come into the likeness of Christ completely. The Sabbath was symbolic. The blood of bulls and goats was symbolic. The blood of Christ is the final offering the prior symbols represented. We are, as believers, a purchased possession, owned and belonging fully and completely, seven days a week, to our Lord and Savior, Jesus.

There were no excuses good enough to break God's Sabbath of the seventh day. Even if there was much work to be done, things needing attention, God still required observance of His Holy interruption. In Exodus 34:21 we read, "Six days thou shalt work, but on the seventh day thou shalt rest: in earing time and in harvest thou shalt rest." In other words, even though the fruit of the harvest needs tending, you will still rest. There likewise is no excuse for our not allowing the constant interruption of the Holy Spirit in our lives. We cannot say, "Oh, I am too busy to yield to God." We cannot say, "Oh, God doesn't understand my problems, they are too many for me to demonstrate love and patience in the situation." We cannot say, "God can't expect me to be loving and kind with that person, they are too difficult to deal with." There simply is no excuse for breaking the Sabbath covenant with God.

Hebrews 4:10 says, "For he that is entered into his rest, he also hath ceased from his own works, as God did from his." As we learn to lay aside the works of the flesh, self-will, self-effort for God, revenge, bitterness and the like, we will abide in His peace and rest. We are told in Matt. 5: 17 that Jesus came to fulfill the law, not destroy it. Jesus was continually challenged by the Jewish leaders of His time because He healed and ministered on the Sabbath. They did not understand that He was demonstrating the fulfilling of the intention of the Sabbath. He was doing the work of God, not His own will or works. He indeed had completely ceased from His own works (own will), and was truly resting in God's Sabbath rest in all that He did.

In John 5:19, Jesus proclaimed that He could do nothing of Himself, but could only do what He saw the Father do. It was the Father's will to heal and help on the Sabbath, and Jesus flowed in that heavenly love and desire. The Father, and Jesus, worked on the Sabbath. But the work was done from a place of resting in God, not human effort. This was God's message in the Sabbath originally, cease from your own ways and honor Me. We, today, honor God's new covenant Sabbath by yielding our self-will and self-works to Him, and learning to walk in His rest, that place of complete obedience to Him in every moment and every matter that touches our lives. It is only through the power of the Holy Spirit that we will find the ability to enter into the place of God's rest. It is through the enlightenment of the Word that we will learn the ways of the Spirit and learn to cooperate with Him as God leads us into His holy rest (Hebrews 4:12).

TRUST ALLOWS PRAISE,
WHICH LEADS TO VICTORY

Heavenly Father, we are greatly encouraged by the truth of Your Word. It is food for our souls, strength for our spirits, and light for our paths. As much as we have sought You, we have only begun to see the riches hidden in the wonders of Scripture. Give us a greater hunger for You, a greater discipline to set aside time alone with You, and increase our understanding through the enlightenment of the Holy Spirit. Cause us to see where before we have been blind and ignorant. Transform our thinking to be in harmony with the thoughts of Jesus. Increase our faith, casting down the strongholds of unbelief and darkness. Glorify Yourself through our lives, Lord, for we offer them up to You. In Jesus's name we pray. Amen.

HE APPOINTED SINGERS UNTO THE LORD...
BEFORE THE ARMY (2 CHRON. 20:21)

Are you challenged? Are you facing difficulty in your life, your body, your family, your profession? Do you at times feel as though an onslaught from an "enemy army" has come against you? Take courage! God has an answer, a victory, and a blessing all wrapped up and ready! Jehoshaphat was challenged with the threat of destruction, death, and possible captivity as a prisoner of war, and God led him through it into a blessing at the other side. He will do the same for us if we believe and seek to obey Him.

In 2 Chronicles 20:2 Jehoshaphat received word that a "great multitude" had come against him and were camped nearby, preparing for war. The challenge had arrived. It looked overwhelming, and it was close at hand. If the Holy Spirit has begun a work in our hearts at all, we will find ourselves in similar situations. For, it is through testing that God accomplishes His transforming work in our lives and brings us into the intended blessing. Upon receiving this word, Jehoshaphat feared. He was worried and concerned, but he was also a man of faith and trusted in God. He immediately set himself to seek God in prayer and fasting (verse 3). The challenge was serious, and Jehoshaphat got serious about seeking God for help. In verses 5-13, we read of the people coming together to pray and seek God. They rehearsed before the Lord the words of God's promise to Israel (verses 8&9). They began to verbalize their trust and belief in the Word of God, quoting it to the Lord in prayer. Then, as we read in verse 12, they cast themselves totally upon the mercy of the Lord. "O our God, wilt thou not judge them? For we have no might against this great company that cometh against us; neither know we what to do: but our eyes are upon Thee." They did not ask God why they were facing this situation—they referred to the Word of God when He said, if this type of thing happens, cry unto Me (verse 9).

We are likewise told in 1 Peter 4:12, "Beloved, think it not strange concerning the fiery trial, which is to try you, as though some strange thing happened unto you." Challenges are destined to come to the "beloved" of God, so we should arm ourselves with the right frame of mind when they come. It does not mean we are not beloved of God; it affirms that we are! It is the enemy of our souls, Satan himself, that seeks to have us take a "woe is me" or "why me" attitude. Self-pity quenches the work of the Holy Spirit and leads to spiritual defeat. We must learn to stand up against the lies of the evil one and trust God when tested.

God then answered Jehoshaphat's prayers by instructing the Israelites to go and face the challenge, march out to the enemy army, an army many times greater than they were. He further told them to not fight, but stand still and see God's salvation, as we read in verses 15-17, "Thus saith the Lord unto you, be not afraid nor dismayed by reason of this great multitude; for the battle is not yours, but God's. Tomorrow go ye down against them: ...Ye shall not need to fight in this battle: set yourselves, stand ye still, and see the salvation of the Lord." So, they prepared to obey God and go forth to face the enemy. And in a show of their faith, (He said to them that they would not fight in the battle) they put the singers in front of the army (II Chron. 20:21). Such a move makes no sense whatsoever to the natural mind, placing the choir in front of the swords! However, this was a tremendous act of faith and a demonstration of their trust in God. Jehoshaphat admonished the people to "believe in the Lord your God, so shall ye be established; believe his prophets, so shall ye prosper" (verse 20). He was telling them to believe in what God had said to them yesterday. He spoke to strengthen their faith, and demonstrated faith by putting the singers first.

The singers were to praise the Lord as they went before the army of Judah toward the enemy. The two words for praise used in verse twenty-one mean to revere and worship, and also to celebrate, shine, make a show, even somewhat foolishly. We then read of the glory of God as He fulfilled His word by destroying the enemy army, as Judah moved forward in faith and trust, as foolish as it looked in the natural. "And when they began to sing and to praise, the Lord set ambushments against the children of Ammon, Moab, and mount Seir, and they were smitten... and everyone helped to destroy another" (verses 22-23). When the army of Judah, and the singers, arrived at the scene we read, "And when Judah came toward the watch tower in the wilderness, they looked unto the multitude, and behold, they were dead bodies fallen to the earth, and none escaped" (verse 24). Verse 25 then tells of the great riches and blessings Judah carried away as the spoils.

If we will put praise and worship between ourselves and our challenges, we will find God coming to our aid just as He did to Judah! As foolish as it sounds, and as difficult as it may be to do, if we will praise and worship God, trust Him completely, and believe that our challenge has no power, we will rejoice to see the day when we come through the difficulty and into the rich blessing of God. When we let go of our own efforts to solve the problems and release them to God, we will find His peace and victory. Jehoshaphat let go in this way by telling the army (the only thing he had in his own power to solve his problem) to follow the singers. He didn't trust in his soldiers; he exercised his faith! He put praise and trust in God between himself and his challenge. 1 Thessalonians 5:18 admonishes us, "In everything give thanks: for this is the will of God in Christ Jesus concerning you." This instruction was demonstrated by Jehoshaphat as he put the praise of God first in the face of a devastating challenge! God does not design or allow challenges to harm or destroy the Christian who walks in faith and is seeking to obey God. He allows only that which He sees is necessary and helpful in leading us into greater blessing, greater spiritual stature, and greater likeness to Jesus. Nothing will frustrate the devil's work more than when the Christian praises God in the midst of difficult times. Such a heart attitude seals us off from the devil's attacks and protects us from the destructive power of adversity.

FINDING CONFIDENCE
TO APPROACH GOD

Heavenly Father, teach us how to pray. Help us overcome the obstacles of unbelief and doubt, and the error of looking at our faults. You saw our weaknesses when you saved us, and by Your Spirit we believe You are working to perfect us. Keep discouragement from becoming a hindrance to our prayers of faith. Let us believe You for the answer to prayer and learn to understand that our faith glorifies You. We are imperfect in many ways, but let our hearts not shrink from praying in faith believing in the face of our flaws. Let our eyes be upon You and Your greatness, and upon Your desire to answer prayer and help. In Jesus's name we pray. Amen.

PRAY IN FAITH, SHUN UNBELIEF, AND
CLAIM OUR RIGHTEOUSNESS IN CHRIST

How do we pray? Are we uncertain of how to approach God? Are we timid in believing Him for an answer? Perhaps we feel unworthy to expect much from Him in our prayers. We struggle with our weaknesses and are very conscious of our shortcomings. We know we are far from perfect. However, these things should not prevent us from boldly approaching God in prayer for ourselves and others. Hebrews 4:15-16 encourages us to come to God in prayer and acknowledges that we have infirmities. "For we have not an high priest which cannot be touched with the feeling of our infirmities; but was in all points tempted like as we are, yet without sin. Let us therefore come boldly unto the throne of grace, that we may obtain mercy, and find grace to help in time of need." Infirmity means weakness, inability to produce results, which is how we often feel in our walk with God, not only physically, but spiritually as well. To begin a walk with God, we must first claim and receive the power of forgiveness He provides for us through the shed blood of Jesus. The blood of Christ is freely given to cleanse and make us righteous in the eyes of God if we will apply it to our hearts by faith. Having done this, then we should not allow the devil to tell us we have no right to come to God or to expect His help. Because of our faith in the atonement of Jesus, we have every right to approach God. Hebrews 10:19-23 states: "Having therefore, brethren, boldness to enter into the holiest by the blood of Jesus... let us draw near with a true heart in full assurance of faith, having our hearts sprinkled from an evil conscience... let us hold fast the profession of our faith without wavering." Here we are encouraged to enter the very holiest, a place where under the law only the high priest was allowed to enter, and then only once per year (Heb.9: 7-14). We need to take hold of the power of forgiveness, accept it, and not waver in our trust in God's cleansing of our sins, His compassion toward our weakness, and His willingness to hear us as He works to perfect us and strengthen us.

He accepts us as we are, while He works to make us into what He sees us to be in Christ.

Those who received from Jesus, came to Him in faith. In Mark 5, the woman who had an issue of blood for twelve years did not say, "Maybe, if He wills, Jesus will heal my sickness." No! She said in her heart, "If I may touch but his clothes, I shall be whole" (Mark 5:28). She was convinced of His ability to heal and knew beyond any doubt that He would heal her. She had released her faith in Him unconditionally and had pressed through the crowd around Him. Weak though she was, she stretched out her hand to touch His clothes. Immediately, she was healed!

In Matt. 14:36, 12:15, and 8:16 we read that all who came to Him were healed. These were not perfect people. They were folks who had struggles and weaknesses just as we have. However, they came believing He would touch them, and He did. In Matt. 13:58 we read: "And he did not many mighty works there because of their unbelief." Satan would have us accept the lies of a spirit of unbelief to prevent us from experiencing the blessings of God. Even Jesus does not move among those who entertain such a spirit. Thoughts such as, I'm not worthy; I don't know enough about the Bible; I have struggles and fall in sin, can provide access for a spirit of unbelief to enter our hearts. We need to take all such thoughts to God, place them under the cleansing blood of Jesus, and accept instantly our forgiveness in order to prevent Satan from quenching faith in our hearts.

In Matt 8:5-13 we read a wonderful story of a Roman soldier who came to Jesus to ask healing for one of his servants. Jesus said He would come and heal him. The soldier then replied: "Lord, I am not worthy that thou shouldest come under my roof: but speak the word only, and my servant shall be healed" (Matt. 8:8). Here we see a person seeking help from Jesus stating, "I am not worthy," but none the less believing! Knowing he was unworthy did not prevent this man from praying that Jesus would heal his servant, and believing in His power to do so. Jesus was so moved by the man's faith that He said: "Verily I say unto you, I have not found so great faith, no, not in Israel" (Matt. 8: 10). Then Jesus said to the soldier: "Go thy way; and as thou hast believed, so be it done unto thee" (Matt. 8: 13). Jesus responded to the man's faith.

In Acts chapter five, verse 16 we read: "There came also a multitude out of the cities round about unto Jerusalem, bringing sick folks, and them which were vexed with unclean spirits: and they were healed every one." People with weaknesses, infirmities, struggles with sin, and all manner of difficulties, were healed, every one! Such is the power of God in response to faith.

Scripture is rich with encouragement to pray believing God for answers and help. In Acts 4:23-31, the believers prayed for boldness to speak the Gospel in the face of persecution, and God was so pleased with the prayer for boldness that the whole building physically shook as they prayed. In James 5:14-16 we read: "Is any sick among you? Let him call for the elders of the church; and let them pray over him, anointing him with oil in the name of the Lord: and the prayer of faith shall save the sick, and the Lord shall raise him up." Continuing, James uses Elijah as an example of someone who had struggles like we have and yet God used his prayers, as we read: "Elias was a man subject to like passions as we are, and he prayed earnestly that it might not rain: and it rained not on the earth by the space of three years and six months" (James 5:17). James 5:16 says: "The effectual fervent prayer of a righteous man availeth much."

Matthew 21:22 reads: "And all things, whatsoever ye shall ask in prayer, believing, ye shall receive." He does not say, he that is perfect and has no struggles shall receive, but he that believes! Finally, let us read the words of Jesus as he encourages us to pray and believe. John 14:12-14 says: "Verily, verily, I say unto you, He that believeth on me, the works that I do shall he do also; and greater works than these shall he do; because I go unto my Father. And whatsoever he shall ask in my name, that will I do, that the Father may be glorified in the Son. If ye shall ask any thing in my name, I will do it." While faith must be balanced with a sincere desire to obey God, these are powerful words of encouragement to pray and believe! We may not understand why all our prayers are not answered as we expect, but we are clearly encouraged to believe God for His touch, His help, and His strength to carry on.

DROP THE EXCUSES,
WE CAN OVERCOME

Heavenly Father, we come to You asking for the inner strength and power to stand in the face of the evil onslaught that comes against us. We ask for alertness of mind to recognize the seeds of evil thought, which seek to bring forth wrong thinking and actions in our lives. We pray for a quickening to resist entertaining them for even a moment. Keep the house of our hearts and minds swept clean and filled with Your thoughts, Your Word, Your vision and purpose, Your love, mercy, and forgiveness. We will step forward to cast out and resist dark influences through Your power and strength within us. In Your name we claim all the authority You have given us over evil. We desire to be holy in the secret places of our lives, Lord, so that we may be worthy of Your blessing and anointing. In Jesus's name we pray. Amen.

WHEN LUST HATH CONCEIVED IT BRINGETH FORTH SIN (JAMES 1:15)

There is a reality of what Satan is attempting to accomplish that, when understood, will help the Christian vehemently resist evil. In many Scriptures God refers to falling into sin, and turning away from Him as spiritual adultery or whoredom. Judges 2:17 tells us, "They went a whoring after other gods." 1 Chronicles 5:25 says, "And they transgressed against the God of their fathers, and went a whoring after the gods of the people of the land..." The word whoring in the Hebrew means to commit adultery. James carries forth a similar concept when he says that when lust hath "conceived" it brings forth sin. God views our relationship to Him as one of marriage. We are referred to as the bride of Christ. Therefore, sin operates to destroy this relationship just as an adulterous act does in an earthly marriage. In the realm of the Spirit, God considers it an act of adultery when we entertain evil, yield to it and bear its fruit. God compares turning from Him, or rebelling against Him, to "playing the harlot," or having intimate relations with someone other than Him.

As Christians, we are the bride of Christ. We are committed to Him in an eternal, spiritual relationship of marriage. God has taken this view since the very beginning. Satan is trying to get illicitly intimate with the Christian, the bride of someone else...the bride of Christ. Sin and evil are conceived when we get too intimate with evil and allow our fallen nature to have its own way.

Not all spiritual adultery manifests itself in acts of outwardly visible sin. Evil conceptions can be multiplied in the thought realm and inner heart attitude. The Lord tells us clearly that He desires that every thought would be brought into subjection to Him and His light (2 Corinthians 10:5). When we are tempted to think thoughts of anger, hatred, bitterness, uncleanness, lust, resentment, impatience, and the like, we are being drawn by Satan and enticed to entertain his seed of darkness, that it might conceive in us and bring forth acts of flesh and darkness. Satan loves to sow his seeds in our lower nature flesh man to further his ways. He tempts us to act or think in wrong ways and then falsely provides justification for our error as he did to Eve (Gen. 3:4-5). Then we find ourselves making excuses just as Adam and Eve did (Gen. 3:12-13). If we begin to see this tactic for what it is, an illicit affair with someone other than our Lord, we can more willfully and strongly resist such an attack. We need to see Satan's temptations for what they are, and scream and shout in defiant resistance as one who was the target of a rapist. Our minds belong to God, and we are not to allow thoughts to take root in us which are not in keeping with the Word of God.

If we protect our hearts and thoughts, then the outward manifestation of evil will not materialize, for outward sin is the result of inner intimacy with the flesh and the devil. Simply put, Satan wants to embrace us, and have us embrace him so that we might give birth to evil and sinful thoughts and actions. His "embraces" are subtle, playing on our weakness and our tendency to justify ourselves. "Well, it is too hard for me." "Certainly, God doesn't expect me to forgive in this situation." "I have a right to do what I want, at least in this matter." Caution! God desires to perfect us in everything. He purposes to bring every one of our thoughts into subjection to Him.

What should our attitude be toward thoughts that come to take root in us which are contrary to God and His Word? A look at the Old Testament commands of God regarding stoning will shed some light on that answer. In Deuteronomy 13:6-11, we are told that God commanded anyone who attempted to entice the children of Israel away from the Lord and into an intimate, secret, relationship with other gods to be killed by stoning. Even if the person was one's brother, wife, or friend, they were to be killed. In Deuteronomy 22:24, we read that this was the way that evil would be put away from among them. God intended His people to purge themselves from evil influences. Stoning was a method that required the people to take an active and aggressive participation in purging the evil. God could have taken the life of the sinner Himself, with no involvement from the people, but He did not and for an important reason. He wanted the people to identify the sin, pick up a stone in their own hand, and cast it at the evil influence.

When was the last time we stood with aggressive posture to cast a stone at the evil influence seeking entrance to our hearts and minds (our thoughts), instead of making excuses for them? The object of stoning was to kill the source of the evil influence. With holy anger they were to stone to death the source of evil. They were not allowed an attitude of, "oh, it's no big deal." In Deuteronomy 13:8 we read, "thou shalt not consent unto him, nor hearken unto him; neither shall thine eye pity him, neither shalt thou spare, neither shalt thou conceal him: but thou shalt surely kill him." This is a very clear instruction to treat the matter seriously, not let it remain hidden (in our minds), but get the sin identified and removed.

This should be our attitude toward anything that draws near to us in thought or outward influence to turn us from the Lord and obedience to Him. The spiritual darkness that tempts us, and the flesh man that would entertain the temptation, are to be cast out and put to death by our own purposed determination and will, and the grace of God. Our flesh must die, and the evil whisperings of Satan must be confronted and cast out.

We need to move away from attitudes of, "I'm so weak and can't seem to get victory over my temptations", or "please pray for me I always fall in my weakness", to a posture of "come near me again you evil influence and you'll get a stone right between the eyes!" It takes willpower and good old determination to resist the evil that surrounds us. And it takes a knowledge of God's Word to know how we should be thinking and acting to recognize the flesh and the devil and turn away from them. We need to see ourselves as new creatures in Christ, and believe we are indeed separated from evil by our rebirth in Jesus and the power of His blood. Then when temptations come, we can know that they are not a part of our new man in Christ, but are coming at us from the enemy who is attempting to entice our old nature flesh.

God expects us to learn to recognize evil and the ways of the flesh, and to take an aggressive posture against them in resistance and determination, just as Israel was required to stone the offender. It is not a sin to be tempted. Jesus was! It is a sin to allow temptations to conceive (to come into existence and expression), either in our thoughts or actions.

PATIENCE AND LONGSUFFERING ARE A SIGN OF GOD'S POWER

Heavenly Father, turn our energy of prayer into a more productive time. May we spend less time praying for ourselves, and more time praying for others. Grant us the grace and strength to live pleasing in Your sight. You know our needs before we ask. Let us trust you with our provision, as it is promised in Your Word. May our focus be on not grieving the Holy Spirit in us with old nature living and self-seeking. May a kind word replace wrath, a loving gesture overcome bitterness, and silence quench the angry spirit. Glorify Your name in and through Your children. Let love be manifest in supernatural power, to draw the errant soul into Your tender care. May the living waters of Your Spirit break forth to refresh the parched and barren thirst of men's hearts. In Jesus's name we pray. Amen.

THAT YE MIGHT WALK WORTHY OF THE LORD (COL. 1:10)

We are taught in Scripture that we of ourselves are not worthy of heaven. A consistent message is that all men have sinned and come short of the glory of God, and that none of us is righteous of ourselves. Man cannot attain salvation, forgiveness of sins, nor eternal life by works, but rather by faith in God and the redemptive work of Jesus on the cross. What then does it mean to walk worthy of the Lord? This statement seems to imply good works on our part to earn His favor or blessings. Perhaps a better way to say it would be, to walk worthy of the Lord, who has already forgiven us, granted us eternal life, and overlooked all of our faults and weaknesses. That is if we have confessed Him as Lord of our lives, confessed we are sinners, and accepted His forgiveness through faith in His death, shed blood, and resurrection. He has already given us so much, we should make every effort to please Him, by learning to walk worthy of His love, grace, and mercy. To walk worthy is to press forward in a walk in the Spirit, seeking His will for our lives, so that our behavior might not embarrass Him by whose name we are called. Thus, to walk worthy is not to earn something from Him, but to become fit to receive and experience all He has already given.

In Colossians 1:9-11 we read, "that ye might be filled with the knowledge of His will in all wisdom and spiritual understanding: that ye might walk worthy of the Lord unto all pleasing, being fruitful in every good work, and increasing in the knowledge of God: strengthened with all might, according to his glorious power, unto all patience and longsuffering with joyfulness:" It takes spiritual understanding to grasp and follow the will of the Lord. I Peter 2:19 tells us to learn how to suffer wrongfully, when we have done nothing to deserve such suffering. Ephesians 5:20 tells us to give thanks for all things, not just the good and pleasurable, but the difficult and challenging as well. There is no way we can learn these graces if we do not embrace spiritual understanding. To our own selves such instruction makes no sense at all. But, in the spirit, much growth is accomplished when we put such things into practice.

We are told to be fruitful in every good work. The fruit that matters is the fruit of the Spirit. This is the fruit that manifests itself in our lives because of the work of the Spirit in the inner man of our hearts. Galatians 5:22 lists the following as fruits of the Spirit: love, joy, peace, long suffering, gentleness, goodness, faith, meekness, temperance. These fruits are to manifest in all of our life, not only on Sunday mornings and prayer meeting nights. In our homes, places of work, daily chores, and all of life is where God seeks to cause these fruits to grow, and when no one else is looking! This revelation of itself is an increase in understanding God's will.

We are also told that we can be "strengthened with all might, according to His glorious power" (Col. 1:11). Hallelujah! We all like the idea of having power and might. Not that we know what to do with it all the time, but it sure sounds good. Yes, Lord, give me some of that power! As we continue in this verse, we discover why we need the power. He says, "unto all patience and longsuffering with joyfulness." To have patience and longsuffering we need His supernatural power. We prefer to not be patient, and we tend to have difficulty suffering long with anything we do not like. In this world of instant gratification, self-seeking, and self-centered living, it takes an extra portion of God's power to keep us from being swept up in the torrent of wrong thinking and self-seeking.

To have patience is to have power! To be longsuffering is to have power! To bear the fruits of the Spirit in the face of pressure, challenge and difficulty is to have power! For we demonstrate that our circumstances have no power over us, and do not control our expression. This is true, empowered Christian living! And then, as we finish this verse, we see again why we need spiritual understanding to accomplish the last admonition... "with joyfulness." We are to have patience and longsuffering with joyfulness. We could rewrite this passage to read, "patience and longsuffering with frustration." Normally, when we are in a situation that tries our patience or requires us to be longsuffering, we can feel frustration swelling up within us. Obviously, frustration is not joy. How then can we find joy in the trying of our patience and in situations that require us to bear long with them? The answer is to gain spiritual understanding. Joy comes to our hearts as we pause to realize, "Lord, is that You?" Yes, He is looking in our hearts to help us respond properly, worthy of Him in every situation. As we realize He is there, working in us, we can find joy in His presence as we recognize His handiwork in our lives. God is out to transform us - from the inside out, and completely. Once we acknowledge His hand at work, His joy comes, and with it comes strength to endure and overcome. Hallelujah! "For the joy of the Lord is your strength" (Nehemiah 8:10).

We are more inclined to pray, "Lord, fix this problem for me." Or "Lord, remove this situation from my life." Or "Lord, please provide me with this or that." Our prayers should be, "Lord take my heart and life and let me show forth fruits of love, patience, forgiveness, kindness, and grace worthy of Your name." If we seek these things, God will take care of the other matters we seem to focus on. In Matthew 6:33, Jesus encourages us to seek the kingdom of God first and all our earthy needs will be met. His kingdom is within our hearts, where Jesus dwells by His Spirit. It is in this area that God desires us to seek Him, making Him Lord over all of our thoughts, actions, and desires. As we understand this and seek to yield to His inner work, we can indeed rejoice in trials of patience, settings of longsuffering, and begin to show forth the fruits of the Spirit. Living a life worthy of the Lord!

TRUE PRAISE IS EXPERIENCED WHEN WE NO LONGER CARE WHAT OTHERS MAY THINK

Heavenly Father, open the eyes of every saint to see the importance of praise and worship. Cause Your Spirit to move mightily as Your people lift their voices, hearts, and hands unto Your great name. May Your praise be continually on our lips, fill our hearts, and be the common thread of all of our thoughts. Great are You, Lord, and greatly to be praised! There is nothing that can touch our lives that should be allowed to come between us and our praise and worship of You. There is joy in Your presence, Lord, and in that joy, there is strength to be a victorious and happy people. Grant us grace to be kept in that wonderful place, regardless of the challenges before us. In Jesus's name we pray. Amen.

THEREFORE, MICHAL ...HAD NO CHILD UNTO THE DAY OF HER DEATH (2 SAM. 6:23)

She was barren! She was to have no children during her life. A harsh penalty, but for what reason? She despised her husband, King David, for his public display of praise (dancing before the Lord) as the ark of God was returning to the City of David. As Michal beheld David dancing in the streets from her window, we read that she "despised him in her heart." That is, she looked upon him as a vile person, a fool, and thought his actions were stupid and base. I am sure he looked rather different than a king at that moment. He had stripped to his undergarments and was leaping with great joy before the ark as it came into the city. It was a time of great celebration as the ark of God was returning to them. In their minds, God was again in their midst! For this they shouted with joy, played the trumpets, and we can assume they also played the other instruments mentioned on the previous attempt to return the ark (See II Sam. 6:5) It was a momentous event with great emotion and joy.

Michal would have no part in it. She did not participate, and scorned her husband for his display of praise. When David returned to his home, Michal met him, and this is what we read: "Then David returned to bless his household. And his wife, Michal, daughter of Saul, came out to meet David and said, "How glorious was the king of Israel today, who stripped himself of his kingly robes and uncovered himself in the eyes of his servants' maids as one of the worthless fellows shamelessly uncovers himself!" (II Sam. 6:20, Amplified Bible). Wow! What a shock. After being so elated and blessed in the presence of the Lord, David walked full speed into a wall of rejection. He was returning to bless his house, while part of his house was prepared to blast him for his behavior. David's response was, "It was before the Lord, who chose me...Therefore will I make merry [in pure enjoyment] before the Lord. I will be still more lightly esteemed than this, and will humble and lower myself in my own sight [and yours]. But by the maids you mentioned, I will be held in honor" (II Sam. 6:21-22 Amplified Bible).

While the king's wife despised David's behavior, David stated that the simple and lowly maids his wife referenced would hold him in honor. They had seen the joy of God in their king. They had participated in the praise and joy of the event. They would hold the behavior of their king in a position of esteem and honor in their minds because he had unashamedly praised, danced, and rejoiced before his God.

There is much we can learn from this story. First, if we are hungry for the Lord, and our hearts are truly seeking to yield to Him, we will unashamedly participate in worship and praise. We will sing, praise, worship, (and, yes, maybe even dance) before our God. While in the presence of others, or alone, it will make no difference if our eyes are upon Him. David said, "it was before the Lord," even though it was in the public streets of the city. Second, if we choose to not participate, and look down upon those who do, we will be barren in the Spirit. There is no way to become a fruitful, powerful Christian without being a person who praises and worships God.

Michal was bound with all manner of "appropriate thinking" about how a king should behave. We may also be bound with similar thoughts about worship that prevent us from entering into the Spirit in worship and praise. Whether it is clapping hands, raising hands, singing forth boldly, singing in the Spirit, or moving one's feet, we should not judge or restrict, but rather, put our eyes on God and rejoice that other are also.

In worship and praise, God moves in the hearts of men to accomplish remarkable things. Burdens are lifted, spirits are refreshed, darkness is scattered, and Satan's oppression is defeated as God's people praise Him. II Chronicles 20 is a glorious story of how praise defeated the enemies of the Lord. In Hebrews 13:15 we are told, "by him therefore let us offer the sacrifice of praise to God continually, that is, the fruit of our lips, giving thanks to his name." David says, in Psalm 122:1, "I was glad when they said unto me, let us go into the house of the Lord." Are we glad when we have opportunity to praise God and enter into His "house" in the Spirit? Are we rejoicing in our hearts when others exhibit extreme joy and blessing in their worship and praise of God? Or do we stand in the window of our minds and despise and question their behavior?

In these days in which we live, it is important that the power of praise and worship be experienced by every believer. This can only happen as we lose ourselves in His presence, as David did in the streets of Jerusalem. Have we experienced worship and praise like David? Have we so entered into His presence in worship that nothing else seems real or relevant as we melt into His love and grace? Have we worshiped in public assembly with our whole heart, leaving nothing in religious reserve? Have we forsaken what others might think of us if we did? Our answer should be yes, and praise God, yes! In such an atmosphere, God is free to minister in wonderful ways. We can be a part of this great ministry of the Holy Spirit, or we can look through our window of scorn and non-participation, as Michal, and remain barren in our heart. The choice is ours.

"After this I beheld, and lo, a great multitude, which no man could number, of all nations, and kindreds, and people, and tongues, stood before the throne, and before the Lamb, clothed with white robes, and palms in their hands; And cried with a loud voice, saying, Salvation to our God which sitteth upon the throne, and unto the Lamb. And all the angels stood round about the throne, and about the elders and the four beasts, and fell before the throne on their faces, and worshiped God, saying, A-men: Blessing, and glory, and wisdom, and thanksgiving, and honour, and power, and might, be unto our God for ever and ever. Amen" (Rev. 7 :9-12).

BITTERNESS HARMS THE ONE WHO ALLOWS IT

Heavenly Father, You are the source of all healing, joy and blessing. It is Your love that seeks to free us from the inner chains and bondage that prevent us from experiencing the fullness of our inheritance as Your children. We ask you to shine Your light of understanding on our hearts and minds so we might see the path to freedom and victory. We ask You to accomplish a quick work in us Lord, for we desire to know You more and live more in Your presence. Remove the roots of bitterness and unforgiveness that hinder our relationship with You and others. Free us into the power of Your love and grace, where we may dwell with You free from the pain and inner torment of hatred and resentment. In Jesus's name we pray. Amen.

IF YOU HAVE ANYTHING AGAINST ANYONE, FORGIVE HIM (MARK 11:25)

When we are hurt, abused (physically or verbally), mistreated, or unfairly dealt with, we are wounded. There is no doubt we feel pain, just as if we hit our finger with a hammer. It hurts and we know it. The severity of the injuries may vary greatly, and some are easier to get over than others. What we need to learn is the reality that if we do not properly deal with the injury, we can be injured yet again (and more severely) if the injury takes root in our hearts as bitterness, hatred, resentment or unforgiveness.

These reactions to hurt are poison to our own hearts from the inside and become more destructive than we may realize.

Being treated unfairly or being abused is like getting a sliver in our finger. A sliver is easily removed and treated in most cases. Forgiving the person who hurt us is like removing the sliver, the wound heals and is of no further problem to us. However, if we do not forgive because of the magnitude of the mistreatment, further damage begins inside us as a result of resentment and evil thinking beginning to take root within our hearts. This is like a sliver, even though removed, (the abuse or mistreatment may have stopped) turning into an infection, which, if not treated, can cause the loss of a limb or even death. We can be greatly damaged by infections. Unforgiveness leads to an infection of sorts in our hearts.

Unforgiveness leads to our own lives hurting others. We, in unforgiveness, become the tool of bitterness, anger, and resentment which hurts others. We can feel captive to hurtful or malignant behavior that impacts many in our lives. We sometimes cannot seem to get free from doing things we hate doing. We can be hindered in having loving relationships with our spouses, family and friends, because of the inner roots of sin (yes, unforgiveness is sin) in our hearts. Jesus said we are to forgive others so our Father can forgive us. We are prevented from receiving the forgiveness of God, and the cleansing that comes with it, if we hold bitterness within us. Mark 11:25-26 reads, "And whenever you stand praying, if you have anything against anyone, forgive him and let it drop (leave it, let it go), in order that your Father Who is in heaven may also forgive you your own failings and shortcomings and let them drop. But if you do not forgive, neither will your Father in heaven forgive your failings and shortcomings." (Amplified Bible)

God sees that if we do not forgive, we can be "twice wounded" by the hurt we experience. Once by the event itself, and a second time by Satan planting a root of bitterness within us. This second wounding has the potential to be far more serious and destructive, to ourselves and to others, if we let this "evil vine of unforgiveness" grow and flow into other relationships. We are to abide in Jesus, His love and forgiveness, not in the evil vine Satan would plant in our hearts through our hurts. We are admonished in Hebrews 12: 15, "Looking diligently lest any man fail of the grace of God; lest any root of bitterness springing up trouble you, and thereby many be defiled." Here we see that the root of bitterness not only troubles us, but many others can be defiled by it also. Why? Because we tend to vent our hatred and anger, affecting many around us in our lives. Also, our relationships with others can be influenced by the infection we carry inwardly, which prevents experiencing the full blessing in marriage, family relationships, friendship, and fellowship with others.

God's love comes to us to heal the infection. We may not be able to avoid the slivers of life, but we can avoid the infection of the devil. Deuteronomy 32:32 speaks about the grapes being bitter and the resulting wine being poison. The "wine" we drink of, and *serve* to others is the expression and outflow of our hearts. If we have "bitter grapes" within, we will partake of and serve "poison wine" to others.

We may be thinking, "Wait a minute! You mean I'm the one who has been wronged, and God says to me that I am to forgive? What about the one who hurt me? I want God to deal with them! It does not seem fair that I must forgive. They deserve God's wrath." This reaction is normal, but does not stand up to Scripture. God knows that if we do not forgive, we will be further damaged, and He wants to spare us from that. Before his crucifixion, Jesus told his disciples, "The prince of this world (Satan) cometh, and hath nothing in me" (John 14:30). In other words, "Satan has no roots planted in me that he can express through. There is nothing in me that Satan has planted, and therefore my expression is free to be only what is of God." We are called to this same standard as His children.

Our lives can be affected in many areas because of wrong heart attitudes springing forth from resentment, unforgiveness, hatred and anger. Relationships, finances, guidance, doors of God's blessing, answers to our prayers and the Lord's help in many areas can be hindered because of the bitterness of our own hearts. We can actually cut ourselves off from His blessings, and miss our "birthright" privileges because of our own wrong thoughts and actions. Jeremiah 4:18 says it well: "Your ways and your doings have procured these things (bad things) for you. This is your wickedness, because it is bitter, because it reaches to your heart." (Amplified Bible) Because the bitterness was all the way to the heart (well past the initial wound of the "sliver") the people had experienced the withdrawal of God's blessing. In verse 14, God commanded them to cleanse their hearts and remove the evil thinking from their minds. Unforgiveness, bitterness, hatred, resentment, all must be removed before we can come into the fullness of God's blessing and joy. Jesus tells us He has come that our "joy might be full" and that His "joy might remain in you" (John 15: 11). Joy comes as we abide in Him (John 15:1-10). And in Him, Satan has nothing - no roots of bitterness and unforgiveness! Let us learn to pray and forgive those who plant their "slivers" in our lives, and refuse to let an infection of bitterness start in our hearts.

HE WAS BORN TO MAKE US VICTORIOUS

Heavenly Father, we celebrate the birth of Jesus, the Savior of the world, and we are moved with concern for those who have not found victory and overcoming life in You. Too many of us struggle in arenas of defeat. Too many of us have failed to take hold of the power and strength You have provided. Our prayer this season is that the joy the angels shared when they proclaimed Your birth will fill the hearts of every believer to overflowing. That where there is defeat, there would be victory. Where there is a slowness to obey, there would be a quick response with great determination to please only You. Where there is confusion and depression, let there be clear wisdom and joy, as Your Word and Spirit fill every heart. May many souls be saved, as they behold the love and joy in the lives of Your people. In Jesus's name we pray. Amen.

FOR TO US A CHILD IS BORN, TO US A SON IS GIVEN (ISAIAH 9:6)

Isaiah foretold of the birth of Jesus Christ, the Savior of those who believe, as we also read in Luke 2:11. Isaiah (in chapter 9) told us that the Lord would be called by the names of "Wonderful Counselor, Mighty God, Everlasting Father, Prince of Peace." He further told us the kingdom of the Lord would be without end, and full of peace. As we follow the birth of Jesus on the first Christmas morning, through His life and ministry, and then observe the coming of the Holy Spirit after Jesus was received up to heaven, we can see it is the intent of God that His church, (all those who believe on Jesus as Lord and Savior) would be victorious over darkness, struggle, and challenge, and bring glory to God! (See Luke 10:19, Romans 8:35-37, I John 5:4, Matthew, 5:16, I Corinthians 6:20.)

Prior to announcing the birth of Jesus, Isaiah (chapter 9) spoke of the great things that would happen when this Child was born. In verses 2-4 he told of people who were blind, ignorant, and in great darkness, seeing a great light. He stated that those who were living in the land of the shadow of death would have a dawning of light. These people of which Isaiah spoke were people who, like you and me, were eternally lost, not knowing the light of God's truth and salvation. They, like we were living in this world under the shadow of death, one foot in the grave, alive only in this life, with no hope of eternal life. The shadow of eternal damnation hung over us, whether we were successful in the world or not, and we were separated from the love of God by our unbelief and rejection of Jesus. Then we saw the truth, through the enlightenment of the Holy Spirit, and we received Jesus as our Savior. We had light! A great light!

Verse three tells of our joy, as men who share in the joys of harvesting their crops after long months of tending them, or of victorious warriors after a life-threatening battle, dividing the spoil of the enemy. They were victors. We too are victors, if we believe in Jesus! Verse four says that the yoke of burdens on our shoulders has been broken, and the rod of our oppressor has been taken away. We have been freed from the past, forgiven of our sins, and lifted from darkness into His glorious light to fellowship with Him. This is the truth and promise of God's Word to every believer. We are free in Christ! We are cleansed of all of our sins, if we have repented and confessed our sins to Him (I John 1:7, 9).

Yet, as we come to this Christmas celebration of the birth of this Son, this one called The Mighty God, the Prince of Peace, there are too many children of God who for some reason have not found inner victory. They do not feel like they are free from the shadow of death. In fact, they feel they are held captive in the darkness of defeat, depression, and struggle. They cannot find the higher ground of peace and victory where the harvest is enjoyed, and the spoils of victory are shared. While having believed in Jesus, the Son, the "yoke that burdens them, the bar across their shoulders, the rod of their oppressor" still prevails to some degree and prevents victorious living. Why? How can this be? Is it that the Mighty God, the Prince of Peace, cannot deliver on His promise? Why are His people still in bondage? Where is deliverance, joy, and overcoming power? Has God failed? Is His Word powerless to bring victory?

If we are honest, these questions are asked by all of us at some time or another in our walk with God. And the answer is always, God has not failed! The difficulty is not with God, but somewhere between us and God. Perhaps there is demonic oppression. Perhaps there is a lack of obedience to what we already know. Perhaps it is our lack of faith, or our entertaining a spirit of unbelief. The problems can be many. The answers are simple, but they do require action on our part. We can pray for help, asking God for divine intervention in our situation, but if we are not obeying what we know to be His path and will, we will not see any further answers from heaven. (See Joshua 1:8, Matthew 7:21, Revelations 22:14.) It is when we obey what we know that we will find God moving to bless and protect. If we drag our feet in disobedience, then we are the cause of our difficulty, not God. If we are oppressed by evil spirits, then we have authority over them in Jesus's name. Are we using that authority? (See Luke 10:17-20.) If we do not believe, we need to ask God to help us, and resist the evil influence of unbelief. (See Mark 9:23-24.) If we are not submitting to God in obedience, and resisting the evil we know is wrong, we need to begin to submit, resist, and stand in the victory Jesus provides for us. (See James 4:7-8.)

We are to be doers of the Word, not hearing it only, but acting on it, putting our feet, mouths, minds and hearts in motion in the direction of what the Word tells us. James 1:22 & 25 tells us "Be ye doers of the word, and not hearers only, deceiving your own selves...But whoso looketh into the perfect law of liberty, and continueth therein, he being not a forgetful hearer, but a doer of the work, this man shall be blessed in his deed." Sometimes it is scary to obey. We cannot see how things will work out if we move out on God's Word alone. We must get over this lie! God will never fail, and He will always honor our faith. In fact, our victory is contingent upon our faith, as we read in I John 5:4, "this is the victory that has overcome the world, even our faith." In Hebrews 11, we read of faith in action. We read of people who moved out on faith and God was with them, without exception, regardless of the outcome. God is faithful! Jesus came to bring forth a glorious church, full of faith, power, love, and grace. This Christmas, let us show Him our love by moving in faith to obey, stand, and proclaim His great salvation and victory over darkness. May many be brought into the celebration of the harvest and victory of the warriors as they see His light, His over coming power, His love, and His victory in our lives!

THE WONDERFUL
BLESSINGS OF PRAISE

Heavenly Father, we are in need of more of Your strength and indwelling presence, that we might overflow with Your life, love, and joy to a world full of pain and despair. You have chosen us to be Your people in this world, Lord, and the eyes of many are upon us. May they see more of You and less of us with each passing hour and day. May we be drawn closer to You so that others may find a clearer and purer vision of who You are. May we spend more time in Your presence so that Your life, power, and love may touch a hurting soul through us today. May Your name be glorified and lifted up in our lives. In Jesus's name we pray. Amen.

WHAT'S THE BIG DEAL WITH
SINGING PRAISE ANYWAY?

Why is it important for the Christian to become comfortable with praising God? Is praise something we can omit from our experience? If we choose not to enter into worship and praise, will we be missing out on anything of importance? If we are not used to singing and worshiping the Lord, should we even bother with it? Isn't it enough to gather for a church meeting and hear others sing?

Psalm 100:4 says, "Enter His gates with thanksgiving and His courts with praise." To help us in this discussion of worship and praise, let us assume that the "gates" are the beginning of approaching God, likened unto entering the gates of a city. We begin to come closer to Him as we enter His gates, the outer boundaries of entering His presence. Then, once in the city, we come even closer by entering His "courts", which could be likened to the courts of the temple. As we follow the flow of this psalm, we begin to draw near God by expressing thanks (entering His gates), and we can draw even closer with praise (entering His courts). There is a real connection between praise and worship and drawing closer to the Lord.

Jesus said if we love Him, we will obey His commandments (John 14:21). In Psalm 150 we are admonished to praise God with just about everything we can get our hands on. Psalm 150 closes with "Let everything that has breath praise the Lord." The Scriptures present a truly clear picture, we should be engaged in the praise of our Lord. We are commanded by the Lord to "love the Lord your God with all your heart and with all your soul and with all your mind and with all your strength" (Mark 12:30). Loving God encompasses many things. Loving God most certainly includes being grateful to Him and expressing that gratefulness in praise and worship. When someone gives us a special gift, we animatedly express our thanks. We verbalize our joy in receiving such a wonderful gift. How much more should the Christian express thanks for receiving eternal life and the very Spirit of God Himself into our hearts?

Interestingly, Mark writes that we are to love God with all of our strength. Why does loving God take strength? Picking up a 20-pound bag of potatoes takes strength. Moving furniture takes strength. Lifting weights takes strength. How does loving God take strength? It takes effort! It is a choice of the will. It is a discipline of the heart that must be utilized and strengthened. It takes strength of will to choose to love God by obeying His Word. Praise and worship are the same way. To love God through praise, worship, and song takes an effort. Have you ever worshiped God in song with all of your strength, from deep in your heart, using your full vocal abilities and breath, actually utilizing physical strength to proclaim your praise? This is one way of loving and worshiping God with all of your strength.

In Hebrews 13: 15 we read, "let us continually offer to God a sacrifice of praise...the fruit of lips that confess his name." In I Peter 2:9 we are told that as a chosen holy people, it is our responsibility to declare the praises of God: "You are a chosen people, a royal priesthood, a holy nation, a people belonging to God, that you may declare the praises of him who called you out of darkness into his wonderful light." If we ignore the privilege of praise, we will not know the blessing of entering closer to the Lord. God will let us dwell within His city limits so to speak, without learning the blessing of praise, but we cannot enter fully into His courts (a deeper intimacy with God) without learning to express praise and worship. Psalm 22:3 (NKJV) states, "You are holy, Who inhabit the praises of Israel." To inhabit is to sit down, to dwell, to remain. God actually dwells in the praise of His people! If He dwells in our praise, it is easy to see why praise allows us to draw closer to Him. If we are hungering for more of God, praise is a good place to start looking for Him.

There is yet another reason to participate in worship, praise, and singing unto the Lord, and that is for the benefit of others. As Christians, we are placed in the body of Christ as a living part of the Church of God, which is His body - a spiritual body of believers. (See I Corinthians chapter 12.) In the body of Christ, there are no spectators. Every part is important to the whole. Every person who touches the life of a Christian should touch the life of Jesus in that believer. We are to be His witnesses in this world, in how we live, how we speak, and how we worship. There is a powerful truth taught through the life of Paul and Silas. The lesson is this, when you and I worship and praise God, the people next to us have the opportunity to be delivered and set free by the Spirit of God. That is right! As we gather together and worship in songs of thanksgiving and praise, and lift our *voices,* others who are yet bound in darkness have an opportunity to be set free.

How can this be? In Acts 16, Paul and Silas were in prison for casting out a devil from a slave girl. After being beaten, they were cast into prison, into an inner cell with their feet fastened in the stocks, the jailer being commanded to guard them carefully. At midnight, bloody and beaten, Paul and Silas prayed and began to sing praises to the Lord (Acts 16:25). The other prisoners listened. (These other prisoners could be likened to people who have not yet decided to follow Jesus, those who may visit a Christian service seeking to know about God, but are yet bound in their sins.) As Paul and Silas praised God, there was a mighty earthquake, all of the prison doors were opened, and everyone's chains were taken off! Not only were Paul and Silas set free from their chains, but every other prisoner around them was also set free. God broke loose every bondage within ear shot of Paul and Silas as they sang and praised God. Amazing! Wonderful! Powerful! Those listening to two Christians singing from their hearts were given the opportunity to go free. Church should be like that! As we gather to worship God, let each one of us put forth all of our strength and determination, loving Him with our praise. May He so fill and inhabit our praise that those yet in the prison of unbelief, doubt, torment, and sin, may be given the opportunity to go free.

When the Holy Spirit was given on the day of Pentecost, observers of the event thought that the believers in Jesus were drunk with wine because of their behavior (Acts 2:13). In Ephesians 5:18-20, we are instructed not be drunk with wine but to be filled with the Spirit instead. Is this an unholy comparison? Not really. It merely demonstrates that when God's people enter into praise and thanksgiving, there is a very real blessing, filling and overflowing that is joyful and powerful. When one is filled with the Spirit it will affect one's behavior. Ephesians 5:19 tells us how to be filled with the Spirit. "Speak to one another with psalms, hymns and spiritual songs. Sing and make music in your heart to the Lord" Here we see that singing, (worship and praise) results in the benefit of being filled with the Spirit, which we are com manded to be!

What type of behavior would one observe in a person who has entered into worship and praise and is filled with the Spirit? Why would some compare it to being drunk? When one is drunk, they do not care what others think of them. So, it is when one is caught up in the Spirit in focused praise and worship. Scripture gives us several examples of physical activity that can occur when a worshiper of God is focused upon the Lord more than his surroundings. Psalm 47:1 tells us that there can be clapping of hands as well as shouts and cries of joy. Psalm 98:4 (KJV) tells us, "Make a joyful noise unto the Lord, all the earth: make a loud noise, and rejoice, and sing praise." Here we see that praise and worship can get loud, joyful, and noisy. Even those who cannot hold a tune well are able to make a loud and joyful noise, which should encourage many of us. Throughout the Psalms, we read of many musical instruments being used to praise God. The harp, the cornet, different types of cymbals, dulcimer, flute, organs, pipes, psalteries, timbrels, and trumpets are all mentioned in the Bible as instruments to be played before the Lord. I think we can conclude that God loves music, especially when it is used to worship Him.

We can begin to see that having a really good time in worship and praise could be cause for others to think we had been drinking. Further, we read in Psalm 63:1-5 (New International Version), "O God, you are my God, earnestly I seek you; my soul thirsts for you, my body longs for you, in a dry and weary land where there is no water. I have seen you in the sanctuary and beheld your power and your glory. Because your love is better than life, my lips will glorify you. I will praise you as long as I live, and in your name, I will lift up my hands. My soul will be satisfied as with the richest of floods; with singing lips my mouth will praise you." As David describes his great yearning for God, he declares that he will lift his hands to the Lord. This is a natural outflow of a heart focused upon God in earnest. This behavior is certainly no stranger than that of a football fan. Imagine what God would do if we praised Him with the intensity of a football fan cheering for his home team in the Super Bowl. If that long pass in the last two minutes is looking like a touchdown, popcorn, soda, arms, hats, and feet are all moving in different directions, as the "fan" is focused only on the ball. Imagine a time of praise when no one in the room was focused upon anything but Jesus. Cares, burdens, doubt, fear, unbelief, sickness, demonic oppression, and disease would all be flying out of the way as we entered the holy presence of God in worship and praise! Psalm 134:2, reads, "Lift up your hands in the sanctuary and praise the Lord." Psalm 141:2 compares the lifting of the hands to a sacrifice, which is a good comparison. It is an act of inner surrender and seeking God which is manifest outwardly, similar to water baptism being an outward act of obedience that is the outflow of an inner heart commitment to the Lord. Therefore, we should not think it strange. (See also I Timothy 2:8.)

Does this mean we must always raise our hands in worship? Better questions are: "Am I so entering God's presence in worship that such activity doesn't bother me," and "am I free to raise my hands in surrender to God?" Our focus should be on the attitude of our hearts, not outward manifestations. Raising our hands, and praising God with all of our strength can be outwardly visible signs of a heart that is truly thirsting after God and seeking to enter His presence in worship. However, deep worship and praise can take place without any visible signs. We should seek to worship with our hearts and minds focused and concerned with God alone, and not on what others might think. Herein lies the key to learning how to worship God in Spirit and in truth... a single-minded determination to praise and worship God until we, like David, can say, "I have seen You in the sanctuary" (Psalm 63:2). If our minds are full of thoughts of the day, worries about tomorrow, or self-consciousness of what others are thinking of us, we are prevented from entering into meaningful worship. It is the attitude of the heart in praise and worship that is important. And it is important not to criticize the physical outflow of heartfelt worship and adoration of God. Our opinions should be lined up with the Word of God.

We must never underestimate the power and importance of singing praise and worship to the Lord. God ministers to His people in great ways in these moments. In II Chronicles 20, we read the story of Jehoshaphat, king of Judah, when Judah was threatened by an army that vastly outnumbered them. The decision was made to put the singers out in front of the army to sing praise (II Chron. 20:21). As they began to sing praise, in the face of pending destruction, the Lord destroyed the enemy army. God moved mightily as His people praised Him. David, the warrior king of Israel, said, "Praise the Lord. How good it is to sing praises to our God, how pleasant and fitting to praise Him!" (Psalm 147:1). David knew the benefits of praise also.

As we gather together to worship, and in our private times with the Lord, let us learn to sing and praise Him with our whole heart. Even if we do not feel like it, and there are challenges that appear certain to destroy us, we will be lifted into His power and comfort through praise as we in faith open our mouths and determine in our hearts to give Him glory. Let us adopt an attitude of determination as described in Habakkuk 3:17-19, "Though the fig tree does not bud and there are not grapes on the vines, though the olive crop fails and the fields produce no food, though there are no sheep in the pen and no cattle in the stalls, yet I will rejoice in the Lord, I will be joyful in God my savior. The Sovereign Lord is my strength; he makes my feet like the feet of a deer; he enables me to go on the heights. For the Director of Music. On my stringed instruments." (English Standard Version) We will be lifted to the heights of blessing as we praise and worship our God!

UNDERSTANDING OUR INNER STRUGGLE

Heavenly Father, we desire to be a people that pleases You, living and acting in ways that bring glory to Your name. We daily wrestle with our own wants and desires, which are not Yours. We desire to live in the Spirit, and yet find it difficult to do so. Lord, we come to You and seek to be filled and controlled by Your Holy Spirit. Deliver us from the ways of our flesh, and strengthen us in the Spirit, to rightly represent Your holy name in our lives. We believe You for Your overcoming power within us, to accomplish that which of ourselves we cannot. Thank You for Your love, patience and strength. In Jesus's name we pray. Amen.

IF I'M REALLY A NEW CREATION IN CHRIST, WHY DO I EXPERIENCE DIFFICULTY IN DOING WHAT I KNOW I SHOULD?

"Therefore, if anyone is in Christ, he is a new creation; the old has gone, the new has come" (II Cor. 5:17). If the old nature, sinful habits and wrong behavior are gone, then why do we fall back into them after we are born again of God? It is believers who experience daily difficulty in fully living up to this passage. Why? To understand this issue, we must first understand how we are constructed. 2 Thessalonians 5:23 states, "may your whole spirit, soul and body be kept blameless at the coming of our Lord Jesus Christ." We are constructed with three primary components, our spirit, our soul, and our body.

The body is most easily understood; it is our flesh body. It is the earthly home of our soul and spirit. In our flesh dwell desires and wants that conflict with our new, born-again nature...things which actually fight against our growth and walk in the Spirit. I Peter 2:11 (KJV) reads, "Abstain from fleshly lusts which war against the soul." Herein is part of our difficulty. We are housed in a body that has wants and desires which war against our eternal soul. The body is also in conflict with the Spirit of God (Gal. 5: 17). The body, as we know it, will not inherit the kingdom of God (I Cor. 15:50). We will receive a new and glorified body as further explained in I Cor. 15: 52-54. Until then, we need to recognize that our flesh, the one we love to feed, rest, and enjoy, has desires and lusts which are not beneficial to our walk in the Lord, and in fact will fight against us.

Our soul, which is eternal, is the seat of our mind, our will, and our emotions. When we are born again our soul is saved or delivered from the penalty of eternal torment and separation from God (Hebrews 10:39). The soul knows, minds (the mind), does or acts out (the will), and feels (the emotions). (See Psalm 139:14, Acts 14:2, Ephesians 6:6, Phil. 1:27, Luke 2:35, Matt. 11:29, Luke 1:46, Numbers 21:4, Psalm 43:5 and 42: 11.) As we will learn, the soul is the area of our existence over which the flesh and the devil seek control, and over which God desires to rule and reign.

Our Spirit is less distinguishable from the soul than the body. However, the Word of God will enlighten us to know the difference between the works of the soul and the spirit, for it is in the Spirit that the Lord desires us to dwell (Hebrews 4:12, Romans 8:1, Galatians 5:16). Our spirit also has awareness, for it confesses Jesus (I John 4:2) and is life to our body (James 2:26). The body, when dead, turns again to dust...it vanishes. It is our soul and spirit which leave the body at death. I Cor. 5:1-2 (Amplified Bible) reads, "For we know that if the tent which is our earthly home is destroyed, we have from God a building, a house not made with hands, eternal in the heavens. Here indeed, in this present abode, body, we sigh and groan inwardly, because we yearn to be clothed over (we yearn to put on our celestial body like a garment, to be fitted out) with our heaving dwelling." Our soul and spirit are eternal, and it is God's desire to have the Holy Spirit influence and control the soul (mind, will, emotions) and put to death the lusts of the body (Romans 8:13, Col. 3:5).

Understanding that the body conflicts with the soul, and with the Lord, helps us to understand why we struggle, in expression and experience, to be what we know we should be. When we are born again, we are born as babes in Christ, not experiencing His fullness yet (I Cor. 3:1-2). We are on a journey of growth and maturing. While we are complete in Christ, we are not fully "grown" in how we behave. The old nature still trips us up at times. (Too many times!) It is similar to the analogy of an acorn and the oak tree. In each acorn is a completely matured oak tree, but it takes time, water, and nutrients to bring this fullness into reality. It is similar in our walk in the Spirit. We are told we are to grow into being mature, up to the whole measure of the fullness of Christ, to grow up into Him in all things (Eph. 4:11-16). This is God's purpose in our lives.

The inner war, which results in our struggling to walk in the Spirit, is for control of our mind, our will, and our emotions. In Romans 7:14-24, Paul describes this inner struggle. He acknowledges that in his flesh dwells no good thing. An admission which is a major step to overcoming our old nature's desires and lusts. In fact, a step that must be taken before we can begin to overcome through the Holy Spirit of God. Paul's words make it clear that the battle over control of our lives does not go away when we are born again. It will most likely intensify, as the Spirit of God comes to cause us to live increasingly in the Spirit, and less in the flesh.

Let us use coffee (the desire for caffeine) as an example. While we are not judging coffee drinkers, of which I am one, this example will help make clear the inner struggle for control. When someone needs coffee to get started each morning, if they do not have it what happens? The body (lower nature, flesh) which is the source of the desire for the caffeine, starts sending the mind (seated in the soul) a signal that it wants something - coffee! The whole focus of life at that moment is being driven by the lower nature "want" of the flesh. What happens next? The mind directs the legs to move in the direction of coffee. Wherever it needs to go, it will go there to get the coffee. The soul in this example has become the servant of the body. The opposite of what God wants. The Lord wants the soul to be controlled by the Word of God and the Spirit of God, and for the body (our earthly tent) to be in submission to the soul and spirit, and ultimately God. And in many cases, if not most the lower nature reacts and acts when wronged with responses not of the Lord, having nothing to do with the physical realm. The metaphor of caffeine can be used to understand lusts and desires in other areas such as pornography, selfishness, and other old nature lusts (Gal. 5:19-21).

Now that we understand the basic factors in the inner struggle, the flesh warring against the soul and being contrary to the Spirit, we can move forward walking in the knowledge of what is taking place inside of us. The importance of admitting that "in us there is no good thing" should not be underestimated. We are offended at this thought. We seek to justify our actions, responses, and weaknesses. We do not like to admit we are wrong. The power of confessing the truth that there is nothing good in us begins to give us understanding into the difference between the flesh and the Spirit. Even honorable and noble actions are not "good" of themselves. If they are seeking to satisfy our pride and ego, then they are seeking to glorify or defend our old nature self and not the Lord. Good works will not earn any soul admission to eternal life, nor will they make a selfish sinful heart clean from the inside.

Satan's lie is to clothe the old nature self with religious and good works, leaving the inside untransformed. Understanding that of ourselves we are not good humbles us and allows us to receive God's righteousness.

Renewed thinking reveals that holy robes placed over an untransformed heart will make us no better than the Pharisees who Jesus said appeared righteous on the outside, but inwardly were full of darkness (Luke 11:39; Matt. 23:26-28). Isaiah confirms this truth in 64:6: "All of us have become like one who is unclean, and all our righteous acts are like filthy rags." Pride is an obstacle we must overcome if we are to walk in the blessings of God (James 4:6 and Luke 18:10-14).

Paul admits that the evil he is struggling with is right within him. It is not someone else who is the problem, the problem lies within his very own old nature! Paul states that "sin dwells in me," and that when he would do good, "evil is present with me." (See Romans 7:20-21.) He further describes the conflict in verses 22-23 as a war going on. If we fail to see the war, we have been deceived by the enemy. It is the evil one who would convince us we are fine and there is no problem! The beginning of overcoming the inner struggle is to acknowledge three things: First, we, of ourselves, are wretched (Romans 7:24). Second, we need to desire to be delivered from the hold our old nature has on us (verse 24). Third, we need to believe and thank God that our deliverance and victory is through Christ in us (verse 25). What happens to us during the "war" within if we stumble and lose some of the battles? Do we lose our salvation? No. We did not earn our salvation by good works, and it cannot be kept by works either! We are saved by grace, which is a gift of God. (See John 10:28-29, Ephesians 2:8-9 and Gal. 3:1-3.) We do not lose our salvation. God does not condemn us either, if our heart's desire is to please Him and obey Him (Romans 8:1). So then should we keep sinning and letting the lower nature control our lives and actions? No! Paul, who had a full understanding of God's grace (which is God's free and unmerited gift of life to us, and forgiveness of all our sins, when we deserved death) addresses the danger of wrong thinking about God's grace in Romans 6:1: "What shall we say, then? Are we to continue in sin that grace may abound? By no means! How can we who died to sin still live in it?" (ESV) Sin always has consequences. While we are forgiven repeatedly, if we confess our sins and seek forgiveness, yet we will suffer the consequences of our actions. If we continue to live with the lower nature in control, we will be robbed of the full blessings of God and of rewards and benefits. II Tim. 2:20-21 speaks of vessels of honor and dishonor, stating that if we cleanse ourselves of dishonorable activities, we will be made useful to the Master and prepared for any good work. Scripture also explains that we will each receive according to what we have done in our bodies, and that some will suffer loss of rewards, although they will be saved (Matt. 16:27 and I Cor. 3:13-15). There is, therefore, great incentive to cooperate with the Holy Spirit in overcoming our fleshly, lower-nature desires. Self is to be put to death (inclusive of our "religious" self), and that takes a determined effort of the will on our part (Romans 8:13 and Col. 3:5), and a yielding to the Spirit of God within us.

We must learn to change the way we think about our old nature before we can be free from it! It is not our friend. It is our enemy. Its lusts and desires are contrary to God's purposes. Romans 12:2 speaks of being transformed by the renewing of our minds. Renewed thinking recognizes the hazards of the flesh and propels us to resist our lower nature demands. And what are these demands? Gal. 5:19 states, "The acts of the sinful nature are obvious: sexual immorality, impurity and debauchery (extreme indulgence of one's appetites); idolatry and witchcraft; hatred, discord, jealousy, fits of rage, selfish ambition, dissensions, factions and envy; drunkenness, orgies, and the like." (Note: the internet is an area of great temptation to some with the ease of access to pornography. God sees in secret, and we must strive to live a holy life in His sight.) We know the areas where our flesh seeks to control us. We need to seek God's grace with a determined will on our part to obtain deliverance and victory in these areas. He is our source of strength, and we can do all things through Christ in us! (See Phil. 4:13.)

Satan also adds to the conflict, as an ally to the lower nature. We are warned that the devil "prowls around like a roaring lion looking for someone to devour" (I Peter 5:8). The evil one loves to encourage us to seek to fulfill the lower nature desires and appetites. He will put temptation in front of us where we are weakest and attack our weakest front. He will add to the cries of our flesh saying, "Surely God doesn't require that of you. Why try and live such a holy life?" His second line of assault is in spiritual deception. If he can't hold us captive in the lower nature, he will seek to deceive us spiritually. This is why it is imperative that we stay before the Lord in prayer, and in the study of His Word. We must be grounded in the truth of the Bible and have a consistent prayer life. This coupled with a teachable spirit and humble heart will give us great advantage over the attacks of the devil.

To put ourselves on the path to overcoming life we need to do three things: 1. Renew our minds with the knowledge of the Word of God (the Bible). 2. Exercise our wills in God's direction saying, "I will, whether I feel like it or not, put my flesh to death and seek your will, spending time to seek your face in prayer and your Word." 3. With a renewed mind and exercising our will, determine to not let our emotions, or other fleshly lusts, control us or our decisions. We should never make a decision when we are in a state of high emotions. The key to greater life in the Lord is increased death to our selfish old nature. Jesus said in John 12:24, "Except a corn of wheat fall into the ground and die, it abideth alone: but if it die, it bringeth forth much fruit." We need to align ourselves with the Holy Spirit in us, choosing to deny the flesh and old nature, as it is He who is working in us to fulfill God's will and purpose (Phil 2:12-13).

DO NOT INVEST IN THE WRONG EFFORTS

Heavenly Father, give us clear understanding of what you require of us. Keep us from pouring our energy into mere earthly pursuits, even though they may be religious. Teach us to invest ourselves into that which pleases You and has eternal benefit. May our thoughts and intent of heart become pleasing to You. In Jesus's name we pray. Amen.

SOLD OUT TO GOD, OR...

The degree of yielding to which we are called is overwhelming. To our selfish nature it sounds most unreasonable. Loving God and believing in Him should be sufficient, shouldn't it? After all, isn't giving Him something better than giving Him nothing? Oh, how shortsighted we are. We fail to see it is through giving all that we receive unmeasurable abundance. Jesus sought to help us understand this principle when He taught that he who would lose his life would find it. It is in yielding that we gain, and in sacrificing that we receive, and that a hundred-fold! The impassioned plea in Romans 12: 1 is brought to bless us, not rob us. We read, "I beseech you therefore, brethren, by the mercies of God, that you present your bodies a living sacrifice, holy, acceptable to God, which is your reasonable service." A total sacrifice of our lives is requested here. But do we understand what this means?

We will misunderstand this command, and walk into destructive behavior, if we fail to apply the very next scripture to the sacrifice. And that is, "And do not be conformed to this world, but be transformed by the renewing of your minds, that you may prove what is that good and acceptable and perfect will of God" (Romans 12:2). There are many folks who make tremendous sacrifices in the world, but to no spiritual benefit, and with destructive consequences. As an example, a person can be "sold out" to his career. Such a person will sacrifice family responsibilities to spouse and children, relationships, and balance for the sake of career advancement. The destruction that follows such sacrifice may well be a family left starving for affection, love and time, which leads to divorce, resentful children with little guidance, physical illness and other stress related ailments. This is a trap many Christians fall into in the name of "selling out to God."

One can sell out to a ministry, or a Christian work, and yet not be properly sold out to the Lord. We can rightly or wrongly live out our "living sacrifice." Paul explains this hazard in I Cor. 13: 1-3 where he says one can be filled with the Spirit, speak in tongues, speak the Word of God (prophesy), have great wisdom, understanding and faith, move mountains, give money to God's work, and even give one's life for the ministry and yet have failed. Paul is saying that a person can be completely absorbed in Christian "things" (call it ministry, church, missions, evangelism, vision, or whatever you wish) and yet have it profit nothing! Do we grasp this? He is saying that love, and its inner fruit in our hearts, is not tied to the outer work of ministry. We need to get ahold of this truth! It is confusing to our goal oriented, prideful selves.

We determine our worth and success in God's sight by what we can see accomplished in the way of outward Christian work. But God looks only upon the heart. If the heart is not right, the works are no better than filthy rags. We tend to want to be very religious, very active in Christian activities, for from this activity we derive a feeling of self-satisfaction that we are laboring for God. We must be careful. Outer activity of itself means nothing. What is in the heart means everything to God.

Jesus confronted this problem in Mark 11:9-13, where some people were dedicating themselves totally to God but forsaking their responsibilities to their parents. Jesus said that such out of balance dedication was "making the Word of God of none effect." God was not pleased with this sacrifice. There is a marked difference between selling out to a vision or work, and selling out to God. We are to be a living sacrifice to the Lord, not to a Christian work. This is where the transforming of our mind comes in. We need to have God's light on the subject of sacrifice. Sacrifice to the Lord will not result in an out of balance selling out to a work, but rather a manifestation of the grace, love and patience of the Lord, and God's priorities in our lives. It will result in a transformed life! A life that will place God's priorities in front of those of the world. To sell out to a career (or ministry) is somewhat expected in the American culture. God says husbands are to love their wives as Christ loved the church, and gave Himself for it. If there is a conflict between family and career, what should we choose? We cannot hide in the excuse "well, my career is providing for my family." God is providing for our family! We need to be obedient to Him. Is God pleased if a wife's heart is devastated by lack of love and affection from her husband who is sold out to career or vision? Not according to Ephesians 5.

Obedience to God will lead to an inner sacrifice often in conflict with the outer, easier sacrifice. To put God and His order as a priority inwardly may require letting go of some of what we feel we must accomplish in our ministry or career. This pains us on the inside. Success, acclaim, being well respected for working extra hard, and the praise of man are all difficult to sacrifice. Sadly, far more difficult to sacrifice than wives, children and family. Why? Because we are fallen in nature, self- seeking, and prideful. The truth hurts, doesn't it?

God will accomplish His ministry only as we put ours into His hands.

When we are in the spirit and not the flesh, there is always time to obey God, love our spouses and children, fulfill our earthly responsibilities, and walk in peace. Scripture tells us that a requirement for ministry is to be able to manage our own households well. If our spouse's heart is broken and our children are starving for attention, Scripture tells us we are not qualified for the ministry (I Tim. 3:2-5, Eph. 6:4). Are we willing to let our minds be transformed in this area? I pray so. When we view family, spouse, children, and time spent with them as "hindering our ability to reach our goals for God or career," or as "frustrating baggage," there is a strong indication that our goals are feeding our flesh ego. We are moving in self-energy and are more important in our own eyes than we should be.

Selling out to God (a living sacrifice) will result in our loving, nurturing, cherishing and valuing our spouses, while working together to raise our children in the ways of the Lord. This may cost us the praise of men (religious Christian men), but it is a true, inner sacrifice that is pleasing to God. There were religious rulers who believed in Jesus's message, yet could not openly confess Him (live a sacrificial life) because they were trapped in the mold of needing the praise of men more than the approval of God (John 12:42-43). Jesus seeks to break the chains which keep us from becoming a God-pleasing, living sacrifice. Accolades from our peers, fear of rejection, fear of not getting a promotion, fear that others will think less of us, these are the things that pollute our concept of a living sacrifice. Being a living sacrifice is not "burning out for a vision or a work" (I Cor. 13:3); it is coming into balance with the Holy Spirit in fulfilling His will and purpose in us. If we are placing our pride, our will, and our desires on the altar inwardly, we will outwardly live a life in balance with the Word of God. The fruit of the Spirit grows in the soil of a heart broken in obedience to God. Brokenness comes from dying to our own wants, desires, visions, self-importance, and pride. Are we willing to sacrifice these things or are we too busy being sold out to something other than God?

HOW OUR HEART ATTITUDE OPENS OUR UNDERSTANDING OF GOD'S WORD

Heavenly Father, we ask for wisdom, understanding and guidance. Help us to have the right heart attitude so that we can receive that for which we ask. Open our spiritual eyes to see that study alone will benefit us to a point, but that yielding our life and will to Yours is the beginning of greater light and understanding. Forgive us for our prideful ignorance and help us to accept Your terms and requirements, for they are before us to lead us to Your rich blessings. In Jesus's name we pray. Amen.

HOW CAN I UNDERSTAND WHAT GOD SAYS AND WHAT HE WANTS OF ME?

Jesus gives us an important key to understanding God and finding truth. But before we look at that key, let us briefly look at how God created man. Genesis 1:26 tells us we are made in the image of God, in God's likeness. God has a mind, a will, and emotions...so do we. We have a free will, just like God has a free will. We can choose and decide what we will do, where we will go, what we will believe and not believe. The cornerstone of this study is about our will and God's will. For, as we will see, this is where the key is hidden to understanding God and discerning truth.

Jesus tells us in John 7:17(Amplified Bible), "If any man desires to do His will (God's pleasure), he will know (have the needed illumination to recognize, and can tell for himself whether the teaching is from God or whether I am speaking from myself." The King James version says it this way: "If any man will do His will, he shall know of the doctrine, whether it be of God, or whether I speak of myself." Thus, the key to knowing is in doing God's will.

Now that we are told what the key is, let's look at what God's will is and what it isn't. Jesus said the pure in heart would see God (Matt.5:8). To see clearly the will of God requires that the inner life, the secret places of our hearts and minds be pure... purged of the old nature and transformed into the likeness of Jesus. Outward service alone will never purify the heart. Our thoughts, desires, resentments, bitterness, anger, and the like must be changed before we can clearly see. Jesus was very clear when he said that religious, church and Christian service fell far short by themselves. Matt. 7:21-23 explained that not everyone who called upon the Lord would enter heaven, but those who did the will of the Father. Some of those who had spoken the Word of God (prophesied), had cast out demons, and had done miracles in the name of the Lord were cast out from the presence of God because He never "knew" them. They had done outward service, but had not known the Lord in the heart. Works and service in the outer can be false. Many appear wearing sheep's clothing, but inwardly (in the heart) they are full of darkness (Matt. 7: 15-16). Jesus said that by their fruits we would know them, not by their outer works. We are easily impressed by outward activity and grandeur when instead we should be trying the spirits to see if the source of the ministry is from the Spirit of God (I John 4:1).

If our lives are a mess and we are untransformed in the heart, then attending a service or doing a Christian deed will only be placing sheep's clothing over the wolf of our old nature. Or to put it a different way, we will be placing a "holy robe" over our untransformed fallen nature.

This is not God's hope for us. He starts His work on the inside and then the outward manifestation becomes real, born from an inner life in line with God. Matthew 6:4-6 speaks of the Father seeing in secret (in the inner places of our hearts and minds) and then rewarding us openly (or outwardly). It is as God does His transforming work in the secret places of our heart that true outward service is born, anointed of His Spirit. To serve outwardly then is, by itself, not God's will for any believer. Rather, to yield inwardly so we bear the fruit of the Spirit, is the beginning of doing God's will. (The fruit of the Spirit is love, joy, peace, patience, kindness, goodness, faithfulness, gentleness, and self-control; Gal. 5:22-23.) Remember, Satan comes as an angel of light. We, too, can look pretty good on the outside in front of others. It is what is on the inside that matters. And those who pay the price of dying to self and yielding to the Lord on the inside, can discern those who have not. There is only one foundation that will withstand the testing and trials of life... the inner foundation of yielding the will to God.

Matthew 7:24-27 tells the story of two men who both built. One built with a solid foundation, the other built on sand. Foundations are unseen. When the testing comes, only that which is built on the inner yielding of the heart to the will of God will stand. All the Christian activity in the world will not add one bit to the inner foundation of the Holy Spirit in us if we do not yield the will to God. We can cover our old self-willed, stubborn, rebellious nature with the best of outer works, but it will not stand in the day of testing and will not help build others in the Spirit.

Yielding the will hurts. When our plans are blocked, when our thinking is challenged by God (through others), when we are treated unfairly, when we wish to strike back, when harsh words break our hearts, when our path is changed to a direction we would not have chosen - this is where the Holy Spirit begins His inner work of transformation, in secret where only God, and you and I, see.

Isaiah 58 tells of exactly the message we are studying. Israel was seeking God daily, asking of Him, delighting in approaching Him, fasting, looking pretty good on the outside. What did God say? "Shew my people their transgressions, and the house of Jacob their sins" God said that their fasting was for selfish motives, finding pleasure (their own will). They had strife and violence in their hearts, and the outward activity did nothing to help the inner problem (58:4). God's answer to the problem was to get them to allow the inner life to change. As we read in Isaiah 58: 13-14 (New King James Version): "If you turn away your foot from the Sabbath, from doing your pleasure on My holy day, and call the Sabbath a delight, the holy day of the Lord honorable, and shall honor Him, not doing your own ways, nor finding your own pleasure, nor speaking your own words, then you shall delight yourself in the Lord; and I will cause you to ride upon the high hills of the earth." The key here is the same as Jesus told us - doing the will of God from the heart will give us sharp vision by which to please God and follow His path. Our own will can be anything from wanting a pathway of blatant sin to wanting to accomplish great exploits for God, but both can carry the same stench of the fleshly and fallen nature.

What is God's will if it isn't outward works alone? It is showing forth the fruits of the Spirit (Matt. 7:16); to humbly show love and mercy and act justly (Micah 6:8); to be joyful and give thanks in all circumstances (I Thessalonians 5:16-17); to love one another (John 15: 12); to love our enemies and those who persecute us (Matt. 5:42-48); and to keep our hearts free from bitterness toward those who may wrong us (Matt. 18:21-22). These are the will of God worked out in the secret recesses of our hearts. From this inner foundational work, outward service will be meaningful, spiritual, and anointed of the Lord. Without this inner work, outward service is only a cheap imitation, mimicked by the fallen nature but lacking the anointing of the Holy Spirit.

There is only one way for our knowledge and understanding to increase, and that is to make room for more of Jesus in our hearts. This requires letting go of more of our selfish nature, pride, ego, rebellion, wrong thinking, unbelief and our stubbornness. All of the treasures of wisdom and knowledge are hidden in Him. The more of Him we allow to live in us, the more our understanding will increase. The will of God is for us to die to ourselves daily, making room for more of Jesus.

SIX PILLARS IN THE FOUNDATION OF FAITH

Heavenly Father, our eyes are upon You, for there is no other to whom we can look for the help and strength we need. You alone can open our understanding, to heal our broken heart, to transform our sinful nature, and change us into the image of Jesus. From You alone comes the refreshing and encouragement that enables us to press on toward our hope in the face of challenge, difficulty, and pain. From You we receive answers to our prayers and the grace to understand them. We proclaim, in the sight of all - both men and angels - how wonderful You are, how great is Your mercy, how boundless is Your love, how precious is the blood of Jesus through which we are cleansed, and how grateful we are to be called by Your name. Thank You for saving our souls!

We are reminded of the importance of seeking to live our lives in such a way, that we would not be ashamed if You were to return at any moment. May all of the moments of our lives be lived with the conscious awareness of Your presence. May we think, speak, and behave as though all was done before You - for it is. In Jesus's name we pray. Amen.

ARE WE BUILDING ON THE RIGHT FOUNDATION?

Paul warned us to be careful about how we build upon our foundation of faith in Jesus Christ. He spoke to the Corinthian believers, telling them he had laid the foundation, and others would build upon that foundation

(I Cor. 3:4-15). Paul knew how he had laid the foundation. He had laid it correctly, and completely, as God had instructed him. Hebrews 6:1 gives us six pillars of a proper foundation for our faith in Christ. If one or more of these is missing in our personal "foundation of faith", then we will not have the full platform upon which the Holy Spirit can construct the likeness of Christ in our hearts. It takes a complete foundation to allow for the full spiritual expression of God to be manifest in each of His children. As we look at each of these six pillars, let us examine our own hearts to see if our foundation is complete.

"Therefore, leaving the discussion of the elementary principles of Christ, let us go on to perfection, not laying again the foundation of repentance from dead works and of faith toward God, of the doctrine of baptisms, of laying on of hands, of resurrection of the dead, and of eternal judgment" (NKJV Hebrews 6:1-2). Here we are clearly given the six foundational teachings for the New Testament believer in Christ. Let us look briefly at each of the six.

Repentance from Dead Works. We begin our spiritual life, the beginning of our eternal salvation, by faith in the gift of God's forgiveness. We are saved from eternal damnation by the grace of God, not by works or self-effort to be better (Ephesians 2:8). However, the idea that our works for God make us accepted of Him easily finds its way back into our hearts. We become those who cover our shortcomings with more works of service. We fall into the trap of doing to make ourselves feel better about ourselves, rather than allowing God to transform us from the inside, which makes us be more like Christ. Being more like Christ is God's intended goal for each believer (Ephesians 4:13). "Doing" is an easier substitution, but may have no eternal benefit. Paul admonished the Galatians to not allow works to take the place of faith and trusting in the Holy Spirit (Gal. 3: 1-11).

James goes on to tell us that faith without works is dead (James 2:17-26). However, faith will lead us to an inner yielding to the Holy Spirit, which will sanctify and anoint our works. These are the works that are alive. Works of service from an untransformed heart are dead. They are the activities of our old fallen nature (the wolf) in sheep's clothing. Many an ambitious ministry effort is fueled by such energy of the flesh... but we are told to try the Spirits and to not be impressed by the outward appearance of things. We are to repent from dead works - ministry efforts and Christian service from our untransformed old nature. We are to shun them, flee from them, and seek rather to inwardly yield to the will of God. Doing so will result in the fruit of the Spirit in our lives. The reason this repentance is so very important is because we remain blinded and deceived if we think Christian service makes us for anger in the home, bitterness toward our spouse, misuse of anger in disciplining our children, verbal abuse, lack of a prayer and devotional life with God, dishonesty, and all manner of other darkness of the heart. This foundational truth is key to allowing the Holy Spirit to build the nature of Christ within our hearts. It is far easier to build in the flesh "for God", serving in Christian work in many different ways, than to yield the will and heart "to God", allowing the Lord to have His will in us.

Faith in God. We are born-again as God's children through faith in the death, atoning blood and resurrection from the dead of the Lord Jesus Christ, God's only begotten Son (John 1:12-13). This is the first step of faith. However, it takes faith in God in countless arenas of life to have a sure foundation. Faith that when things go wrong, God is still in control and has not forsaken us (Psalm 34:19, I Peter 1:6-9 & 4:12). Faith that the power of the indwelling Holy Spirit can give us victory over the weakness and sinfulness of our flesh. Faith that we are worthy in God's sight to receive all of His promises - because of our faith, not our works or goodness (we have none!). Faith that no matter what our background, no matter what scars we carry from past mistreatments, we can be free from bondage and walk in the newness and power of the Holy Spirit - free from the condemnation of the devil. Faith that we have authority over all the power of the enemy, and in Jesus's name we can drive the devil from our lives and refuse to accept his lies. Faith that we wear white robes in God's sight! Robes given us by faith in the cleansing blood of Jesus (Rev. 7:14). Faith that no matter what life's experiences may bring us, no matter how painful they may be, God knows, God cares, and though we may not understand at the moment, God will reveal his eternal purposes in His time (Hebrews 11). Faith that His thoughts toward us are only for our good, never for our harm (Jeremiah 29: 11). Complete faith in God's love for us is the foundational faith we need.

The Doctrine of Baptisms. This foundational truth speaks of plural baptisms. For the New Testament believer there are two baptisms - baptism in water and the baptism of the Holy Spirit. Water baptism is the outward act of obedience to Jesus's command (Matt. 28:19) which mirrors the inner yielding to Him in the heart (Col. 2:12). Phillip baptized the Ethiopian eunuch after his confession of faith in Jesus (Acts 8:36-38). Peter commanded Cornelius, and those with him who had received the baptism of the Holy Spirit, to be baptized in water (Acts 10:44-48). Following the Lord in water baptism is a powerful spiritual experience that should be part of every believer's foundation in Christ. While children may be dedicated to the Lord at very young ages, water baptism should be an act of obedience by those who are old enough to make a conscious decision to follow God in this way.

The baptism of the Holy Spirit is the second baptism for the Christian. From the examples given us in Scripture, it is clear that the Holy Spirit baptism is not one and the same with believing unto salvation. In Acts 8, Philip preached the Gospel to those in Samaria. They believed and were baptized in water. Then, when the apostles in Jerusalem heard this wonderful news, they sent Peter and John to pray for them to receive the Holy Spirit. This was after they had believed, experienced salvation, and been baptized in water. Jesus commanded the first believers to wait until they had received the power of the Holy Spirit baptism before entering into ministry (Acts 1:4-8). Today, the believer needs this same power to live an effective and fruitful Christian life.

As we look at the record of Holy Spirit baptisms in Scripture, we find consistently the manifestation of the gift of speaking in an unknown tongue (Acts 2:4; 10:44-48; 19:1-6). This gift of edification is a special blessing which the Holy Spirit baptism provides for prayer, intercession, and the building up of the believer (Acts 14:4; 14:14-18: Jude 20; Romans 8:26). Having once received the loosening of our tongues to speak in this language (which our natural mind does not understand), we should take care to exercise this gift often. Paul stated his personal practice of praying in tongues more than others (I Cor. 4:18). This should be an encouragement for all believers to seek and utilize this gift. Holy Spirit baptism was not optional for the early church. In fact, we find the apostles seeking to make sure that new converts had received the Holy Spirit, just as they had. Peter, John, and Paul all demonstrated that the new believers should receive the Holy Spirit baptism, as this was the command of Jesus for His church. It was the baptism of the Holy Spirit, as witnessed by the gift of tongues, which convinced Peter that God had indeed poured out His Spirit on the gentiles (Acts 10:44-48 and Acts 15:7-9). It is through the Holy Spirit baptism that God empowers the believer for service in the Spirit, enabling Him to elevate ministry above the best efforts of the flesh. Both water and Holy Spirit baptism are necessary pillars for a sound foundation in Christ.

The Laying on of Hands. The practice of praying for, or blessing others while placing one's hands upon them is an age-old biblical practice. God has ordained the ministry of the laying on of hands as one of the ways the Holy Spirit touches the needs of others. In Acts 6:6, the apostles laid hands on those selected for certain ministry roles as they prayed for them. We find, in Acts 19:6, that the Holy Spirit baptism was received when Paul laid hands on those for whom he was praying. Healing was ministered through the laying on of hands in Acts 28:8. Jesus said that the believers would "lay hands on the sick and they shall recover" (Mark 16: 18). The placing of hands upon another for prayer is an act of faith that God has chosen to honor. Human hands cannot heal, give the Baptism, anoint, nor deliver from evil spirits. However, the prayer of faith, accompanied by the act of faith of laying on of hands, is a manner in which the Holy Spirit can minister to others. While the laying on of hands is not the only way in which the Holy Spirit can minister to others, it is yet an important practice that is placed in the foundational structure of our faith in Scripture (Hebrews 6:1-2).

The Resurrection of the Dead. All men will rise from the dead once to stand before the Lord. However, while the grave is not the end for anyone, the correct understanding of the resurrection of the dead reveals the false teaching of reincarnation, where we are given many different lifetimes to develop and learn. Such false teaching is one way Satan removes the urgency of getting our hearts right today. Scripture states, "do not marvel at this; for the hour is coming in which all who are in the graves will hear his voice and come forth: those who have done good, to the resurrection of life, and those who have done evil to the resurrection of condemnation (John 5:28-29)." (See also Matthew 25:32-41.) Hebrews 9:27 says, "It is appointed unto men once to die, but after this the judgment." We are given one life in which to come to accept the salvation offered us through the sacrifice of Jesus on the cross. If we reject God's love and forgiveness, then our resurrection to face judgment will result in eternal damnation. One life, one death, one resurrection from the dead, and then the judgment. This foundational truth places urgency on pleasing God now, before whom we will stand after death.

Eternal Judgment. There is a day of accountability for each person. Revelation 20: 11-15 states, "Then I saw a great white throne and Him who sat on it, from whose face the earth and the heaven fled away... And I saw the dead, small and great, standing before God, and books were opened. And another book was opened, which is the Book of Life. And the dead were judged according to their works, by the things which were written in the books....And they were judged, each one according to his works... And anyone not found written in the Book of Life was cast into the lake of fire." Only those washed in the blood of Jesus are written in the Book of Life. I John 2:28 speaks of living in a manner that will allow us to not be ashamed before Him. Jesus spoke of some of His servants receiving punishment for not doing the will of the Lord (Luke 12:47-48). It is clear that we will give an answer for our lives. We will be judged.

Yes, we are cleansed of our sins through the blood of Jesus. However, we will also give answer for how we have spent our lives. II Cor. 5:8-10 reads, "willing rather to be absent from the body, and to be present with the Lord. Wherefore we labour, that, whether present or absent, we may be accepted of him. For we must all appear before the judgment seat of Christ; that every one may receive the things done in his body, according to that he hath done, whether it be good or bad." Properly understanding this foundational truth, will place the correct godly fear and reverence in our hearts, and lead to seeking to live a life holy and pleasing to Him - today (Col 1:22).

In conclusion, let us examine our hearts to assure that our foundation is in line with these Scriptures. To effectively walk in the Spirit, we need to have in place all six of these components of our faith. And from there, may we move forward in our walk with Jesus and cooperate with His work to transform us into His image.

BECOMING FREE FROM SATAN'S LIES

Heavenly Father, we ask You for help in learning to walk in the power of faith - a faith that proclaims Your promises over our lives in the face of even the most devastating challenge. We seek the strength of spirit to overcome the lies of the devil and to stand in confidence in the promises of Your Word. By faith we shall stand, and it is our faith that needs to be increased. Open our eyes to the reality of the unshakable ground upon which we can stand through faith in Your Word. Surer is our foundation in the Scriptures than the most solid granite mountain. Cause us to know this with confidence. Grant us the strength to lay hold of the promises You have given us, that we might walk upon this earth as Your children, confident in Your love and care. We praise You and thank You for Your Word and Your faithfulness to us. In Jesus's name we pray. Amen.

LEARNING TO EXPECT GOD'S GOODNESS

The Christian often finds himself asking, "How can I have joy and peace when so many things challenge my life?" The answer is simple. We find peace and joy when we hear from God. In Mark 4:36-41 the disciples were in a life-threatening situation. They asked the Lord, "Carest thou not that we perish?" They were not experiencing peace nor joy, but rather the torment of wondering if God cared for them or not. Their circumstance brought them to this point of questioning the Lord's care for them. When they heard the Lord speak "peace be still" to their stormy circumstance, then they had peace. We too will have peace when we hear from the Lord in our storm. To hear from Him requires faith in His Word and hope in His good intentions toward us as His children. It is through the truth of His Word that we will hear from Him when we believe that which we read applies to us - and it most certainly does!

We will now look at the application of faith and hope, two important ingredients to achieving joy and peace in our lives, regardless of what we pass through in the way of difficulties and challenges.

Hope

David said in Psalm 38:15, "For in thee, 0 Lord, do I hope: thou wilt hear, 0 Lord my God." To hope is to wait, be patient and trust. Webster's defines hope as "a feeling that what is wanted will happen; desire accompanied by expectation." Hope then is a looking forward expectantly. We need to look at our hearts and ask, "How do I look forward?" Do we look forward with confidence in positive expectation of how God will meet our needs and help us? Regardless of the challenge we are facing, we can find joy in the fact that God will help and answer prayer, and therefore we look forward to how He will do it. We look forward to many things in life: a new job, a raise in pay, a new car, a new home, or a gift at Christmas. Though we may not have them yet, we look forward expectantly to a day when we will. We need to apply the same "hope" in believing God to help us and answer our prayers. In paraphrasing Psalm 38: 15, David is really saying, "In You Lord, I will look forward expecting my desires and needs to be met, because you will hear me." David learned to confess these hopes to God in the face of many terrible challenges. What a wonderful statement of hope! One we should claim as our own and confess with our hearts and voices before the Lord.

Faith

Scripture defines faith as, "the substance of things hoped for, the evidence of things not seen" (Hebrews 11: 1). Faith says we have the answers even though we do not see them yet in the natural. Faith is the proof, the reality we have in us that God is there, He hears our prayers, we do not need to see anything with my natural eyes because we see this proof in the Spirit. We see them as a reality in our hope and trust in God, but they have not yet been manifested in the realm of the seen. One proof of faith is the joy and peace we can experience in the now of life, even though the manifestation of our hope is not realized in our circumstances yet. Faith then is confidence in God and in His good and loving intentions toward me as His child. It is confidence in His Word, even though I do not see the fullness of its promise right now in the natural. Faith and hope lift us into the realm of "all things are possible" and the realm of answered prayer. When we can look forward expecting God to answer (hope), and have the faith to believe He will, then we receive the evidence of joy now, today.

We are walking in faith when we can claim God's answers before our eyes see them. We then act like they are ours now, and receive the joy of such confidence. This is walking in the realm of the unseen and not allowing the natural world's circumstances to control our heart's attitude. God promises us His rewards if we believe. As we read in Hebrews 11:6, "Without faith it is impossible to please him: for he that cometh to God must believe that he is, and that he is a rewarder of them that diligently seek him." When we believe He is a rewarder of His people (including each of us!) we join with the people of faith, such as Job, who could say, "though He slay me, yet will I trust Him," and Habakkuk, who said that though his outward world crumble, and there be no fruit from the field, and no flocks in the fold, "yet I will rejoice in the Lord, I will joy in the God of my salvation!" (Job 13:15; Habakkuk 3:17-18) As our difficulties and challenges bring us to this place of trust and abandonment to God, and the tasting of such rich hope and faith, let us thank God for each and every one of them!

Experiencing Victory

How can we experience the reality of this joy, peace, and confidence in God? We must hear from God ourselves. And this will happen when we seek for Him with our whole heart. This is a personal matter between each of us and God. No one else can cause us to hear from Him. We must be the seekers of His face in order to hear from Him. Are we hungering for answers, for help, for victory in our challenges, for confidence in God and His Word? We then must seek Him personally. Attending church services and prayer meetings will not suffice. We must seek him alone, in the solitude of personal prayer, worship, and meditation. Scripture tells us we will find Him. The condition on this promise is that of seeking for Him with all of our heart. "Thou shalt find Him, if thou seek him with all thy heart and with all thy soul," (Deuteronomy 4:29).

Overcoming Satan's Lies

The path to finding Him, and hearing from Him, is not without opposition. To experience the joy of faith and hope we must overcome the devil's lies. Scripture speaks of Satan as being the father of lies and the accuser of our brethren (John 8:44; Rev. 12:10). Satan seeks to separate us from our rightful standing, which is expecting God's goodness with hope and faith. He does this through torment. But the devil's torment is a lie! If we listen to his lies, fear, anxiety, and lack of confidence in God will flood our hearts. Some of the lies Satan hurls our way sound like this: "God is not with you;" "God has left you because you are not worthy of His help;" "You are hopelessly defeated;" "You will never be healed;" "This mess is all your fault, so God will not help you;" "Your own mistakes got you here, and God will never help you now." We must never let such lies of the devil quench our hope and faith in God. King David, even when he was wrong and had sinned, admitted his sin while fervently seeking the face of God to protect him, help him, and keep him from those who would hurt him (Psalm 38). This was the seedbed for hope and faith which lifted him out of his despair regarding his own sin and wrong, as well as the outward challenges he faced.

What we believe matters greatly. Do we accept God's promises and refuse to believe the lies of the devil, or do we wallow in self-pity when things go wrong? Scripture teaches that we are righteous in the sight of God because of our faith in Jesus (Phil. 3:9). Therefore, we are worthy of all God has offered us. Jesus promises to be with us always, to the end of the earth, and that it is the Father's good pleasure to give us the kingdom (Luke 12:32; Matt. 28:20). Do we believe this? If we do, then we should make no room for the lies of Satan that would deny us the heritage of the children of God. According to our faith it will be done unto us. Let us put our faith in His Word and His promises to us (Matt: 9:29). If we cannot expectantly look forward to how God will answer our prayers and deliver us from our present challenges, then the lie of the devil has entered somewhere to cut us off from the joy and peace of God. Recognize this and rebuke the lie.

Prayer Is Required

Prayer and intercession are necessary to break free from Satan's lies. We all have hurt, suffering, illness, needs, heartbreak, and despair in our lives. We need to pray until we come to the place of joyfully and confidently looking forward to what God will do about these things. This is a very real place! It is a place of victory in the Spirit that we experience in our hearts before we see the change in our outward circumstance (which may change quickly, or may not). David referred to God as his refuge and high tower (II Sam. 22:3). A high tower depicts a place of safety, far above the threat below. Sometimes it takes praying, one step at a time, until we ascend this high tower. High towers have many stairs; this can mean many prayers! There is a battle before there is a victory. Our victory is found in the Spirit before it is experienced in the natural. A war is going on and it takes prayer with our whole heart and strength to overcome the devil's lies. Satan is releasing a flood of unbelief and lies to quench our faith and hope in God, to steal our joy, and to prevent us from looking forward with hope. We need to learn to confess in the face of every obstacle and challenge, "Lord, I am looking forward to how You will help and answer my prayer, and bring me through this experience. I thank you in advance for what You are going to do, and what you are already doing right now in the Spirit on my behalf." Victory is assured for those who find this place of faith and hope!

Are We Holding Hands with The Devil When We Pray?

How do we ask in our prayers to God? Do we ask and doubt He will answer? Do we ask and worry about what will happen? Do we ask but really do not believe He will do anything? Do we ask, but believe we are not worthy, so He will not answer? In all these types of prayer there is neither joy nor peace. In fact, when we ask in these ways, we are actually holding hands with the devil as we pray. We are reaching toward and asking of God with one hand, while we embrace one of Satan's lies with the other. Such prayer robs us of victory, joy and peace. We are encouraged in Scripture to pray with confidence and to believe God will answer. We must pray holding the hands of faith and hope, which leaves us no hand free to embrace a lie from the devil. Two Scriptures that lay a sound foundation for prayer are I John 5:14-15 and Mark 11:24. "And this is the confidence that we have in him, that, if we ask any thing according to his will, he heareth us: and if we know that he hear us, whatsoever we ask, we know that we have the petitions that we desired of him." (His Word reveals His will.) "Therefore, I say unto you, what things soever ye desire, when ye pray, believe that ye receive them, and ye shall have them." As we take these promises into our personal lives of prayer, we can experience the victory of God in every circumstance.

Testing Develops Strength and Leads to Great Spiritual Rewards

There are times when God allows torment to touch us, in order to teach us how to pray and intercede in faith. David tells us of the depths of his inner pain and suffering as he walked through many different difficulties and challenges. During these experiences he was torn apart, overwhelmed, and devastated, yet continued to press on with God in prayer. David cried out in Psalm 55:4-5, "My heart is sore pained within me: and the terrors of death are fallen upon me. Fearfulness and trembling are come upon me, and horror hath overwhelmed me." And again, in Psalm 69:3, "I am weary of my crying: my throat is dried: mine eyes fail while I wait for my God." Often it takes much prayer and intercession to God, crying out with the whole heart, before we are lifted free from the lies and torment of the evil one. David speaks of such persistent prayer in Psalm 55: 17: "Evening and morning, and at noon, will I pray, and cry aloud: and he shall hear my voice." David learned to rise to the place of victory through his prayers to God. He found such great confidence in God's answers and help that he says assuredly in Psalm 55:22, "Cast thy burden upon the Lord, and he shall sustain thee: he shall never suffer the righteous to be moved." In other words, He will never allow you to slip, be shaken, fall, waver or fall into decay. Never! What confidence. What peace. Praise God! David's testing led him to a great confidence in God.

What is the result of learning to pray and intercede before God with our whole heart? We will learn to live life expectantly as we eagerly look forward, not fearing the future, nor worrying over our challenges, but rejoicing today in what God will do and is doing in the Spirit. We will gain great confidence in God personally. We will have the confidence David experienced in Psalms 55 and 69, where after pouring out his heart he ended in praise and thanksgiving, confident of the Lord's help. Finding this place of looking forward expectantly does not mean our situation has changed yet, but we have the victory in our hearts and the joy of expectantly looking forward to what God will do. Satan wants us focused on our problems. God wants us looking forward to how He will bring us through. God desires our trust, and He will never... never...let us down!

The Rewards of Faith and Hope

Faith and hope allow us to have the joy of answered prayer before our natural eyes see it. They enable us to say, "I praise and thank God for how He will answer my prayers. I praise Him and thank Him for my needs being met. I praise and thank Him for my healing. I look forward to getting up tomorrow to see what God will do to answer my prayers. I look forward to how God will bring me through this challenge." And we can proclaim all these things with true joy of heart in expectation of our loving Father's help! This is a spiritual reality separate from whatever the outward answer is.

In Psalm 43:5, David talked to himself, encouraging his own soul to hope in God and not be cast down. And in Psalm 16:9 he said, "My flesh shall rest in hope." We too will find rest when we can look forward expectantly and confidently to what God will do for us. Total trust, faith and hope are what God desires for our hearts. This is what Phil. 4:6-7 teaches us. "Be careful for nothing; but in everything by prayer and supplication with thanksgiving let your requests be made known unto God. And the peace of God, which passeth all understanding, shall keep your hearts and minds through Christ Jesus." When we get ahold of this truth, the reality of it, nothing can stop us from looking forward to what God has for us tomorrow.

Paul, facing prison and persecution, says in Acts 20:22-24, "And now, behold, I go bound in the spirit unto Jerusalem, not knowing the things that shall befall me there: save that the Holy Ghost witnesseth in every city, saying that bonds and afflictions abide me. But none of these things move me, neither count I my life dear unto myself, so that I might finish my course with joy, and the ministry, which I have received of the Lord Jesus...." This was spoken by the man who was convinced, and confident, that nothing could separate him from the love of God (Romans 8:38-39).

Whatever lay before Paul on the morrow, he was confident of God's love, provision, purpose, and plan and he looked forward with joy to completing the days he was given, regardless of the setting, be it prison, persecution, or freedom. The things of the world had faded away in comparison to what Paul was seeing in the Spirit. He was abiding in the realm of the unseen - the realm of faith and hope. In this realm there is no defeat for the Christian, only the victory and resurrection power of God.

God is on the throne. He is Lord of heaven and earth. We can only find peace and joy as we become blind to the challenges and setting in the natural and allow faith and hope to propel us to seek Him, believe Him, and trust in Him for our care, our needs, our healing, our deliverance, our protection, and our guidance. Trusting Him, believing Him, and looking forward to His help in the face of our challenges, destroys the power of any circumstance to torment us. Faith and hope close the door on Satan's lies. "For we walk by faith, not by sight" I Cor. 5:7).

SOME OF GOD'S GREATEST TASTED DISCOURAGEMENT

Heavenly Father, thank you for Your unfailing love. Thank you for Your faithfulness and commitment to us who are called by Your name. Praise You that when we are weak, You come to help us. When we are discouraged, You comfort us. When we feel empty with despair, You remind us of the undergirding of Your Word of promise - a promise that will never fail. When the waters rise about us, even as the flood of the enemy, and we feel certain that all is lost, You gently lift our eyes to the unmovable truths of Your Word and lovingly say to our spirits, "rise, walk, and trust in Me, for I will never allow you to be destroyed!" Thank You for Your tender mercy and compassion upon us, for in them we have learned to trust. Thank you that in every situation we can say, "I will hope in My God, for He will never forsake me!" We worship you, praise You, and thank You for Your care and faithfulness. In Jesus's name we pray. Amen.

RESURRECTION FROM THE BITTER WATERS OF DESPAIR

Despair is not uncommon to the saint. Therefore, we should not feel condemned if we find that we are tasting of its bitter waters. Have you been there? Have your feet trod through the desolate land of barren dreams? Have you felt the blast of the hot desert sands blowing continually to blind your vision, until you can no longer see the way? Have you found yourself thinking you must have completely failed God, and because of this failure you are now suffering at the merciless hand of condemnation and despair? Has so much come against you in life that you feel it is simply too much and you cannot bear it any longer? Has your heart cried out, "it is not worth going on"? Do not despair. You are highly likely on the path that follows Jesus. The hand of God is certainly upon you, as He accomplishes His inner work in your heart, and as He works to break your fascination with all things in the outer, that your faith might rest in Him alone.

We should not assume we have done anything wrong because we find ourselves feeling hopeless. Paul, as mighty a man of faith as he was, found himself feeling hopeless, doomed to die, completely discouraged. Listen to his words in II Cor. 1:8 (Amplified Version.), "For we do not want you to be uninformed, brethren, about the affliction and oppressing distress which befell us in Asia, how we were so utterly and unbearably weighed down and crushed that we despaired even of life itself." Paul was there! He was taken to this place of total despair as he walked in service of the Lord. Paul - a man called, anointed, and mightily used of God - found himself drinking of the waters of despair. He was tested beyond his abilities and strengths by the purposeful wisdom of God. When we enter the waters of despair, our hearts likely ask, "What purpose and what wisdom? What good comes to me that I must taste of despair?"

Paul answers this question briefly, yet profoundly, in II Cor. 1:9, where he says, "We felt within ourselves that we had received the very sentence of death, but that was to keep us from trusting in and depending on ourselves instead of on God Who raises the dead." When we are faced with challenges well within the measure of our own abilities to overcome, we feel comfortable, annoyed perhaps, pressed to rise to meet the challenge, yet confident we can handle the matter. This is quite different than being challenged well beyond our abilities and resources. As we look at such an overwhelming challenge, we come quickly to the place of a realistic assessment which says, "This is well beyond me. I cannot handle this. It will surely overcome me. I have no power or ability of my own to manage this, and I feel helpless and in great distress."

Having reached this place of utter despair, we find the fertile ground for faith. While our own assessment in the natural comes up helpless and overwhelmed, yet in the Spirit we have entered that place of opportunity. That place where "all things are possible." That place where our feet are on the edge of the Red Sea, destruction pressing hard behind us, and we have no way to help ourselves. God then says, "Go forth!" And as we do, we look back to find the threat itself destroyed and our feet upon safe and hallowed ground!

Paul said the reason God allowed him to taste of despair was to cause him not to trust in his own abilities, but in God alone. When all else as a source of help is removed, we then find what God has wanted us to learn all along - He is there, and He will deliver us! Paul states in II Cor. 1:10 the wonderful conclusion to his experience of despair: "For it is He who rescued and saved us from such a perilous death, and He will still rescue and save us; in and on Him we have set our hope (our joyful and confident expectation) that He will again deliver us (from danger and destruction and draw us to himself." (Amplified Bible) Thank You, Lord.

How does God look upon us when we are in our times of despair? When our hearts are discouraged and the challenges seem overwhelming? Is He angry? Is He annoyed at our lack of faith? Should we expect His wrath and judgment because of our frailness and ignorance? When we feel we cannot continue another day, should we expect Him to snuff us out with more difficulty and overwhelming challenges... to wash His hands of our unworthy selves? Oh, how we err if we accept such condemning lies of the devil. Paul found God to be his deliverer om his times of despair. And another great man of God found Him to be the gentle comforter.

Elijah was a mighty man of God. A man who is held up to us in James 5:17 as an example as to the power of prayer by a righteous man. A man the Bible says was, "subject to like passions as we are." Elijah had his own experience with total despair. His came after he was mightily used of God to perform the miracles of multiplying food (I Kings 17:11-16); raising a child from the dead (I Kings 17:22); calling fire from heaven (I Kings 18:38). Elijah felt he was the only person left who was standing up for God and His ways (I Kings 19:10). When his life was threatened, he fled (I Kings 19: 1-3). After running one full day into the wilderness, he rested under a juniper tree and prayed that he might die, he could not go any further. "It is enough," he said. What was God's response? Anger? Wrath? Rebuke? No! God sent angels to cook for Elijah and to bring him water to drink. After he had rested, the angel came a second time to feed and strengthen him.

God's purpose for us is to feed and strengthen us so that we can continue. Growth comes when we are challenged beyond our abilities. It is a good thing, and the wisdom of God, which brings us to these times. It is through them we will find God's comfort and provision. And we will grow in our trust in Him when there is nothing else we can look to. Elijah went on, in the strength of God's comfort, to fulfill his ministry. He anointed two kings, anointed his successor, and was taken to heaven in a chariot of fire - the exit of a man in God's favor. A man who had tasted of despair, found God's comfort in it, and continued in the renewed strength he had received. Paul's words, "to keep us from trusting in and depending on ourselves instead of on God who raises the dead," speak to the purpose and wisdom of God in times of despair. When we feel "dead in despair" let us remember we serve a God who "raises the dead." Hallelujah!

LEARNING TO TRAVEL LIGHT

Heavenly Father, grant us the strength and perseverance to resist the assaults of Satan against our minds and our faith. Make us to be strong of spirit, mighty in faith, and disciplined of mind, while learning the joys of becoming children in our complete trust of You. For all eternity we will rejoice in Your presence and the joys of heaven... let that rejoicing begin today! Let the wells of salvation flow with joy to our hearts and overflow to all around us. In Jesus's name we pray. Amen.

DETERMINE TO LIVE WITH JOY

Have you found yourself wishing you did not have certain things in your life? Things, which of themselves should be a blessing? Has concern and worry over certain matters so overshadowed the initial blessings that you would just as soon not have them anymore? Have you found yourself asking God why some of the blessings for which you previously prayed have now become a source of worry and anxiety? Perhaps your employment, your children, your financial standing, family relationships, or your home have begun to burden you beyond your capacity to enjoy them as God intends. What has gone wrong? Why are so many blessed believers so very unhappy and burdened? Where is the joy of God's salvation?

The most simplistic answer is: When a person has nothing, there is little to worry about. This is the blessed state of young children. They have little responsibility, little to oversee and concern themselves with, and this results in a spontaneous joy in living. As we grow and experience added dimension to our lives in the form of responsibilities and blessings received, the challenge to remain joyful increases. We pray for blessings, and then when we receive them, we worry over losing them. We rejoice in family and children, yet carry concern over their safety and their decisions in life. Such concerns may overshadow the joys of the blessings and relationships.

We pray for material blessings and provision, and too easily find ourselves worrying about their continuance and stability. And then we wonder why we have little joy and rejoicing. Learning to rejoice when we have responsibilities, blessings, and favor with God, is part of our Christian growth. We must learn to become as little children in heart, while we grow to increased stature in Christ.

One of the fruits of the Spirit is joy. We know from the Lord Himself that He desires us to have His joy in us, and that our joy might be full (John 15: 11). Satan, on the other hand, desires to rob us of our joy. Why? Because inward joy is our source of strength! We are told that the joy of the Lord is our strength (Neh. 8:10). There is also a connection between a joyful heart and physical health; as Isaiah 66: 14 says: "your heart shall rejoice, and your bones shall flourish." The enemy of our souls desires us to be miserable and weak; taking our joy accomplishes this. As others look at our lives, if the Christians they behold are unhappy miserable people, there is no reason for them to consider following Jesus. Joy is a powerful ally, and one worthy of preserving. How can we learn to preserve our joy? The fruit of the Spirit is a result of God's Word dwelling richly within us. It is from understanding and operating in the truth of the Word that we will find joy sustained.

Jesus spoke of the Word falling among thorns (Luke 8: 14). When this happened, He said the Word was choked and produced no fruit...no joy. Specifically, Jesus said the Word was choked by "cares, riches, and pleasures of this life." The thorns of care and anxiety overgrew the truth of the Word; its power to bring joy and strength were stifled. These cares take root in our minds. It is here we must learn to rid ourselves of them, so the Word can bring forth the fruit of the Spirit within our hearts. I Peter 5:7 presents the concise way to accomplish this: "Casting all your care upon Him, for He careth for you." What are these cares? Care means a troubled or burdened state of mind, worry, concern. The words of Jesus about cares carry the idea of a distraction, anxiety, and apprehension. His use of the word choked means to strangle completely, to drown, to stifle by drowning or overgrowth. This is precisely what happens! Cares and concerns take root in our minds as we listen to them and ponder them. Before long, the power of God's Word to bring hope and joy has been strangled and overgrown to the point that we feel overwhelmed, overburdened, and hopeless. We need to understand what is happening if our joy has disappeared, and take action to regain it!

We are admonished in Luke 21:34 (AMP), "Take heed to yourselves and be on your guard, lest your hearts be overburdened and depressed (weighed down) with... worldly worries and cares pertaining to [the business of] this life." Coupled with Peter's command to "cast all of your care upon Him," we have a formula for retaining joy. It takes action on our part. We are to be on guard and aware of our own thoughts. When the lies of the devil assail us, we are to recognize them and resist them. We are to cast our cares on the Lord because they can become distractions to our hope in His Word. It is like taking the garbage out. If we never empty our homes of the garbage, soon something smells pretty bad. It is the daily removal of the refuse that allows our homes to remain habitable and an enjoyable place to live. It is the same with our minds. We need to daily, and sometimes many times a day, take the garbage of care and anxiety out! We need to throw it out! We need to pray, let go of concern, and trust God.

When we feel overburdened, strangled, suffocated as though spiritually we cannot breathe, we need to know that God is desirous of setting us free. It is not that God wants to take the blessing away, as though the blessing had become a curse, but rather that He wants our spirits free, unfettered from the cares and concerns that rob us of our joy. Philippians 4:6 tells us to "be careful for nothing." This is a command. If we disobey by allowing our minds to dwell on cares and concerns that distract us from thinking upon the truths of God's Word, then we will reap the result of depression and strangled joy. We must work to discipline our minds to think upon the Word in the face of every cause for concern.

Isaiah 12:3 tells us we will "with joy draw waters out of the wells of salvation." And Jeremiah 15:16 says, "Thy words were found, and I did eat them; and thy word was unto me the joy and rejoicing of mine heart." For us to experience our Christian heritage of joy and rejoicing, we must keep our minds free from cares that overgrow the truth. How? By focusing on the Word of God. By reading and reciting it to our own souls. We do not need to focus on the weeds of anxiety to remove them, we need to resist thinking upon them and think upon the Word. What we allow ourselves to dwell upon in our thought life governs our state of being - joyful or distraught. We are told to gird up our loins, the loins of our minds (Eph. 6:14; Peter 1:13). That means to make our minds ready, be alert, be on guard to resist carrying burdens and concerns. This does not mean we should run from our responsibilities, but keep our minds stayed on the Words and promises of God. We need to keep our mental house clean from the garbage of concern, worry and anxiety. Trusting His Word, praising Him in all things, and offering to Him thanksgiving with our whole heart, will keep our minds free and our spirits rejoicing. (Phil. 4:6)!

THIS IS NO ORDINARY RELIGION

Heavenly Father; forgive us for not honoring the Holy Spirit. We have reduced His significance, and our need for His fullness, through our determined self-wills and reliance upon our own power of reason. Forgive us. May we be granted the grace to worship and honor His presence in our hearts, His very holy, indwelling presence. May we be swift to yield to Him in every moment. May we allow Him full access to our expression and ministry. May we have the sensitivity and discernment to know when we have grieved or quenched Him, and move swiftly to correct our transgression, whether in thought, word or deed. May we be found to allow Him full access and control, that we may be pleasing in Your sight. For You Father, are one God - God the Father, God the Son, and God the Holy Spirit. In Jesus's name we pray. Amen.

GOD THE HOLY SPIRIT

Jesus said it was a good thing that He would go away, because if He went away the Comforter, God the Holy Spirit, would come (John 16: 7). Jesus finalized His work on earth by suffering the death of crucifixion followed by the power of the resurrection. Jesus departed in power and glory when He returned to the Father. Following Jesus's departure, God the Holy Spirit came in power with mighty signs and wonders. Not only is the Holy

Spirit the comforter, but also the anointer, the teacher, the revealer of truth, the giver of spiritual gifts.

How do we look upon the Holy Spirit? What importance do we really place upon His presence, His ministry, His intentions? Do we view Him as a less significant member of the Trinity of God? How much do we rely upon Him in all that we do? It is easy to give lip service to God, and then take things into our own hands. It is easy to forge ahead in our own wills and ignore the Holy Spirit. And He will not force us to yield and obey. However, He will not allow our willfulness to go unchecked. He is God. He is God dwelling within the believer to accomplish His will and intentions (Phil. 2:13). If we diminish His significance in any way, we cannot escape the corrections which will surely follow. Yielding to His fullness is not optional!

When the Holy Spirit, and His manifestations are quenched, diminished, or dismissed as not needed, the will and mind of man become the prevailing forces. This is not God's intention. When Jesus raised Lazarus from the dead, many people believed on Him. They had seen the power of God. They accepted the miracle, as hard as it was to understand with the natural mind. Others did not believe, but went to tell the religious authorities what Jesus had done. What did they think? Trickery? Witchcraft? This manifestation of God's power was beyond their religious practice. It did not fit into their patterns nor the comfortable norm. Therefore, they rejected it. Some of those rejecting Jesus were in positions of authority within an accepted religious structure. They viewed the powerful ministry of Jesus as a threat to that which they "ruled" over, that which they controlled (John 11:48). It is when we build in the flesh, the natural, and self-will that we are threatened by the Holy Spirit, for we fear losing control. Control is what the Holy Spirit desires, and can be what we fear to surrender. It is only in yielding control to Him that we will find our lives empowered with the life of God - God the Holy Spirit.

We desperately need to allow the Holy Spirit to control our lives, actions, ministry, hearts, and minds. This means we must surrender control. This is difficult. We seek to stay in control. When the Holy Spirit indwells the heart of a believer, He will not force us to surrender, but He will continue to help us do so. He will allow things to develop that will bring us to surrender. We must acknowledge Him as God, God the Holy Spirit. We must seek to receive His fullness and rely upon His gifts and empowerment for living and ministry. We need His baptism! A baptism of death to our own wills and of yielding to His. A baptism of the natural surrendering to the supernatural. A baptism that loosens our tongues to worship and pray in the language of angels. Such wonders are reserved for those who yield control to the Spirit.

And the one who seeks the pathway of yielding is the recipient of God's blessings. Jesus spoke of the believers having a river of living water flowing out of their inner most being. Scripture clarifies that Jesus was referencing the Holy Spirit (John 7:39). We are to have this source of refreshing and life within our own hearts. Yet many folks fail to develop this innermost well of life, and seek to run from fountain to fountain, constantly sipping at the waters of others, rather than finding the real source of refreshing from God the Holy Spirit within. Which is what teaching should cultivate.

It is easier to allow "this preacher" or "this message" to become a substitute for digging deeper with God personally and finding the lasting source of faith, encouragement, and insight. It is easy to tell when we have yet to fully develop the ability to draw living water from the well of God within us. The words from our lips lift up one person after another, one sermon after another, but fail to speak of Jesus and God the Holy Spirit as the source of comfort and enlightenment. Yes, the preachers are Christian, and the sermons are biblical, yet the true Source, God the Holy Spirit is diminished. A sip from someone else's fountain will not sustain us very long before we are seeking another sip. Once we find the true Source of living water within us, we will be like the woman at the well to whom Jesus said, "Whosoever drinketh of this water shall thirst again: but whosoever drinketh of the water that I shall give him shall never thirst; but the water that I shall give him shall be in him a well of water springing up into everlasting life" (John 4:13-14). This well is discovered in the private devotional life of the believer. It is kept flowing through faith and trust in God the Holy Spirit. We do well to ask ourselves if we have substituted anything else for the true well of God within us.

Properly honoring the work of the indwelling Spirit of God will help us walk in obedience. If we have grieved Him, we need to seek sensitivity to recognize this. If we have chosen a path that is not His will for us, or have allowed our self-will to control our decisions, the Holy Spirit will return us to that point of disobedience. And sometimes that takes years, as he works to enlighten our thinking and help us hear His still small voice. He will work to help us see our mistake. Once recognized, the hurdle of obeying can seem insurmountable. Once we realize there is no escaping the lessons we are scheduled to learn, we can better muster the strength to correct our error.

Peace and blessed release will follow our acts of obedience. We only defer our blessing by dragging our feet. We will become free from the bondage of disobedience as we determine to do that which God reveals. And we cannot compare ourselves with another, for God requires us each to obey on the matters He brings before us. God assures us His blessing, as we determine to obey with the fullness of our understanding. "Oh, that there were such a heart in them, that they would fear me, and keep all my commandments always, that it might be well with them, and with their children forever."(Deut. 5:29).

NOTHING TOUCHES US THAT IS NOT FOR OUR BENEFIT-PRAISING GOD WILL LET US SEE THIS CLEARLY

Heavenly Father, may we find that blessed holy dwelling wherein we find grace and strength to praise *You always. When evil and darkness press in upon* us, *and the enemy assails our souls, may we meet them face to face with* praise *and worship. May we learn quickly, and not forget, the power and victory which is* ours as we stand in the courts of worship and *praise. Pray we must, trusting and waiting are also required, but let us not forfeit the blessedness of* praise *continually through all things. Help us to see and experience that through* praise *we are more than victors over every challenge and difficulty. In Jesus's name we pray. Amen.*

PRAISE GOD AND YOU WILL BREATHE HEAVEN'S AIR

Sometimes things seem to go from bad to worse. Prolonged difficulties and challenges wear on the soul. Unresolved circumstances have a way of growing in weight and concern as time passes. We may be doing everything correctly to the best of our understanding and ability, and yet there seems to be a cloud that covers us - a threatening storm which lingers. Days turn into weeks, then to months, then to years with no apparent relinquishing of the pressure. Why? To what purpose is all of this? Oh, yes, there is a purpose! We must never lose sight of the truth that God's hand is upon each of his children to accomplish His good will and pleasure in and through us. And yes, we often do not understand the present "why" of the matter. Neither did Joseph. From favored son to being sold as a slave, and then to be falsely imprisoned in a foreign land, the why of Joseph's circumstances was withheld for many years...many years.

There is something about adversity that is spiritually beautiful and powerful. Somehow, in the pull and tug of difficulty, stress and challenge, we are shaped and molded to look a little more like Jesus. Our flesh and self-will are crucified a bit more and we are humbled and reduced to worship and praise. Reduced to praise and worship, for we have prayed every conceivable prayer about the matter. We have reasoned with God and presented our case to Him with the detail and passion of the best lawyer. We are forced to rest our case. All we have left to do is lift our eyes in humble acknowledgment that He is on the throne... He is in control. We must yield to Him... and therefore we worship.

What a glorious purpose! That we could be emptied and brought to that place of worship and praise for our Lord in the midst of great and persevering difficulties. What a testimony to the reality of His Spirit within the believer! From this place, we can see the foolishness of doubting that God has a purpose in everything He allows to touch our lives. His answers are best - always! Our problem is that we are too entwined in obtaining our own answers from God... the ones we think are correct. God desires us to be devoted to Him, and trusting Him, as He takes us through many different situations.

If we do not see the answer to our prayers as we desire, what do we do next? Do we accept the lie of condemnation that we are unworthy for God to answer our prayers? Do we become disillusioned with God and doubt that He hears us? Do we allow our faith to falter and entertain the tragic thought of turning our backs on Him? Do we muck around in frustration? Or do we worship? Do we lay it all down and lift our hearts in praise in the face of our problems? This is the calling of the saints! This is the noble behavior the Spirit of the living God within us desires to produce. This is the will of God (Hebrews 13: 15).

In Acts 16, Paul, being grieved in the spirit, cast a spirit of divination out of a young woman. For this, he and Silas were captured and brought before the rulers, being accused of causing trouble. For setting a woman free from this spirit they were arrested. After a severe beating, they were cast into prison. And because the command to keep them imprisoned was made with great emphasis, the jailer thrust them into the inner prison and fastened their feet in the stocks. How rapidly things deteriorated. Why had God allowed this? What purpose could there be to it all? These are logical questions when we observe Paul's situation. But the most important question is what did Paul and Silas do next? They had no control over what had happened to them. But how they reacted next was within their control. So, what did they do? "At midnight Paul and Silas prayed, and sang praises unto God." What was there left to do? They were reduced to being helpless over their circumstance. They were at the end of their own abilities to set themselves free. Therefore, they lifted their eyes and voices to God and praised Him! They did not complain. They did not doubt. They did not fail in faith. They worshiped!

As the pressure increased, and the circumstances deteriorated, from the strange workings of adversity came the glorious fruit of praise and faith in God. Paul and Silas were pressed and molded into a greater likeness to Jesus through the suffering they were enduring. To endure suffering, to embrace adversity, these are unwanted companions for most folks. However, they should be respected and understood by the saints! When we have prayed, trusted, and waited, we must not stop there. We must proceed to the highest proclamation of our trust in God - we must worship (I Chron. 20:20-22). For though we may yet be in the "prison" of unchanged surroundings and circumstances, our spirits can be soaring above it all if we will worship God in the Spirit.

As Paul and Silas praised God, the doors of the prison were opened, and their captor fell at their feet. Their wounds were washed, and the jailer found faith in Christ and was baptized. Still not free to go, they had been ministered to physically following praise to God, and the Spirit of God had ministered to others through them - though they were wounded and still prisoners. Though our circumstances may leave us wounded, or in one form of prison or another, God knows the purpose of it all. There is no prison, no adversity, which can harm or destroy the praising saint. We will most quickly find our victory of heart as we praise and worship Him in the face of all things! Today, praise God!

I WILL STAND AND PRAISE YOUR NAME
(Lyrics by Lex Adams)

I will stand and praise Your name, I will bless You Lord,

I will stand and praise Your name, I will bless You Lord,

When I do not understand why I should suffer so,

I will stand and lift my voice, and let all heaven know,

That I will stand and praise Your name, I will bless You Lord,

Though You slay me, oh, my King, I will bless You more.

When the burdens and the cares, seem too heavy to bear,

I will sing your praise, Oh Lord, I will breathe heaven's air.

GIVE THE OLD MIND
A REST, AND WE WILL
HEAR FROM GOD

Heavenly Father, teach us to employ our minds with meditations on Your Word. Help us to rest our thoughts, which weary us with the constant re-thinking of so much that touches our lives. We expend far too much strength with mental reasoning in the pursuit of direction and self-preservation. Give us the grace to rest in Your peace and trust You. Teach us the blessedness of release - not a negligent approach to responsibility, but release and trust in Your faithfulness, mercy, and care for us. In Jesus's name we pray. Amen.

GUIDANCE... FIND PEACE AND
THE PATH WILL BE CLEAR

In the complexity of matters with which we contend daily, we are often in search of guidance. What should we do or not do? Decisions must be made regarding family, business, ministry, personal finances. Strategy - what strategy should we employ in dealing with an issue? If we make this decision, then what will so and so do? How should I react then? If our lives become like an endless game of chess, we can grow weary in our attempt to make the perfect decision, to protect ourselves from "checkmate." And what if we should make a mistake and decide incorrectly in a given matter?

Oh, how our minds can get moving in their brilliant carnality and leave our hearts in a state of severe unrest. It is true, to be carnally minded is death (Rom. 8:6). While it is an active death, in which we are busy working and plotting things out, it is yet a death to hearing the voice of the Spirit, and death to God's peace within. God is patient with our feeble attempts to orchestrate our own blessing, protection and advantage. Manipulation, no matter how noble or righteous the motive, is flesh and not Spirit.

While it is appropriate to consider the consequences of our decisions and to weigh the pros and cons of a matter, yet we must place a priority on prayer and on seeking the mind of God on every issue. This should be the final deciding factor in all that we do and contemplate. The approach of trying to figure things out in our own minds, exercising our own reason in an effort to protect ourselves, separate from seeking the will of the Spirit, is the wrong approach for the believer. There is another focus which is required if we are to discern the mind of God in any matter. That focus is peace. Not a focus on figuring everything out. Not a focus on weighing all of the information and arriving at a decision, much as a computer would process input data to reach a conclusion, but a focus on finding peace in our hearts and following the decision that brings and sustains that peace.

This decision may be in direct conflict with the "best" decision our own minds can reach in the natural. For we cannot always discern the future and the unforeseen, which could make the best "natural mind" decision the absolute worst one for us to choose. Psalm 34:14 states, "Seek peace and pursue it." It does not say, "seek out every possible outcome and decide upon the best one." Seek peace! This is a spiritual command that will bring us into harmony with the will of the Lord. Employing the best of carnal reason will fail to obtain this goal. Seeking peace does not mean a life free from challenge. It means learning to find and dwell in a place of peace during the storms of life.

Col. 3:15 reads, "Let the peace of God rule in your hearts." To rule is to arbitrate, to govern, to function as an umpire. When our minds are frustrated in our pursuit of the best decision, or in how to save ourselves from a threatening situation, God tells us to let peace govern. What decision brings inner peace to your soul? That is the one God tells us to choose. A helpful guideline is if there is no peace, make no decision until there is. If one decision yields you a better advantage or position, yet brings no peace, it is probably not the correct decision. The decision that brings inner peace is the one from God. (Inner peace does not mean that outer challenge will vanish.)

There is often an inner struggle over making decisions. We are always tempted to make the decision that benefits us personally the most. Thus, in the process of seeking guidance we can find conflict. Conflict between our flesh and the Spirit. And our flesh can put forth a compelling argument for agreeing with it. James 4 tells of wars and fights coming from our desire for pleasure, our lust to have, to covet and to obtain. This coveting can be for material advantage or gain, control, revenge, and a host of other twisted motives. James speaks of asking incorrectly and not receiving because we ask to satisfy our own pleasures. It is when we seek guidance with the willingness to lay everything down and give the Lord complete control over our lives that we will find the peace of God guiding us into the correct decision. The guidance of the Lord will not always seem the best way to our natural mind. We may be giving up things that our flesh desires to seek and keep. Greed and selfishness can come looking very justified - to our own minds.

It is as we let go of that which we seek to control that we will find God opening His doors of guidance and direction. If we fear loss - loss of control, loss of possessions, loss of position, loss of money - then the fact that we fear this loss is compelling evidence we are too connected to the thing in our hearts. When we can release to God that which we fear to lose, we will find our hearts and minds in a position to hear and receive the guidance of God and His peace. If we find ourselves mentally laboring, worrying and consternating *over* an issue, this is again convincing evidence we have not released the matter into the Lord's hands. Until we fully release the outcome of all things into His control, we prevent Him from moving on our behalf in the matter.

When something is important to us, something for which we have worked hard, invested ourselves and our resources into, and care greatly about, it is not easy to release this into God's hands. We can easily be too invested in the subject and get all wrapped up in how we can prevail in the challenge, solve the problem, and navigate to victory. It is our natural inclination to take the challenge into our own minds, rather than to place the matter with God. Sure, we know He is there, but we still prefer to reason our way to a safe harbor. This is often to the neglect of seeking peace and pursuing it. We must remember that our journey is one of spiritual importance, with eternal rewards and consequences. We have all seen the bumper sticker that reads, "He who dies with the most toys wins." We must not forget that it is in losing we gain, and in dying we find life. This is in direct opposition to the views of the world and the flesh. It is when we learn to release the results of every issue into the Lord's control that we truly gain in our spiritual growth and learn to let peace rule. God lifts us into His resurrection life and joy as we learn this lesson. For it is not in the outer results of any matter that we gain or lose. It is whether we have walked in the Spirit, letting peace rule in our hearts which decides our true reward and illuminates our path with the will of God.

TRUST HIM, NO MATTER WHAT

Heavenly Father, help us to be constantly on guard against any whisper of doubt or unbelief that would seek an entrance into our thinking. Without exception, You are in control of every circumstance and moment of our lives. Help us find true rest in this truth. May our eyes be always upon You and our minds meditating only upon Your Word. For in so doing, we will reap the benefit of dwelling in Your peace and find the undergirding of Your joy. Vigilance is required in this, Lord, for in an instant we can slip and find ourselves in the torment of doubt and unbelief. Help us to remain quickened to Your Spirit within us in all things. Oh, Lord, we seek to dwell in the "heaven" of Your abiding presence today, in each moment. Grant us the grace to stand by faith so that this is a reality in the "now" of our walk with You. In Jesus's name we pray. Amen.

TO EXPERIENCE PEACE AND JOY, WE MUST FIRST MASTER TRUST

As believers in God, we too often dwell in torment of mind and soul when we should be dwelling in the peace and joy of the Lord. We see approaching or threatening storms and are bothered. Our hearts are not at peace. We fear. Even though we have experienced God's help in times past, yet the reality of what we are facing can throw us into a state of worry and doubt. We may place the blame for our present challenge on the assault of the evil one, and while he indeed may be on the attack, the root problem may well be within our own heart and mind. Inner peace and joy are not intended to be reserved for a future heaven, but for our lives now, constantly, and amid challenge. Finding them is a worthy pursuit that benefits not only us, but many others and brings joy to the heart of God.

Peace and joy are not obtainable without trust: trust in God, in His Word, and in the fact that He loves and cares for us with a faithfulness and fervency hard to fathom. So intense is His concern for us that He sent Jesus, His own son, to cleanse us from our sins, washing them away in His own precious blood. And this, so that He might have fellowship with us, and we with Him. Because we wrestle with the acceptance of such unmerited love, we open the door to doubt. Doubt which says, "God may feel that way for others, but not for me." This falsehood will prevent any lasting peace, and shut off the fountain of God's joy by weakening the foundations of trust. We must trust Him on His terms, and they include complete, unmerited acceptance because of faith in His Son and His Word. False humility does not impress God; it cuts us off from His fullness. We are clean in His sight if we have believed in the Son of God and His sacrifice and resurrection. We must stand in this position of belief to be able to trust God, otherwise there is no basis for our expecting to receive His promises and protection. Proverbs 3: 6-7 reads, "Trust in the Lord with all your heart; and lean not on your own understanding. In all your ways acknowledge Him, and He shall direct your paths." He shall direct your paths! God does not say He might direct, or will sometimes direct, but He shall direct our paths. It is when we believe this completely that we can begin to experience peace and joy.

Isaiah 26:3 gives us a clear connection between trust and peace, saying, "You will keep him in perfect peace, whose mind is stayed on You, because he trusts in You." Peace of heart is the result of faith thinking. Thinking in accordance with the Word of God. Thinking that relies upon and trusts in what God says, regardless of the volume of evidence we may see in the natural that would seem to make such trust foolish. How we think has a direct affect upon our peace and joy. We must develop the discipline of keeping our minds (our thoughts, our mind's eye) on God and on what He says in His Word. And we must learn to do this in the face of whatever challenge may enter our life. Is this easy? No! But it is simple, and it is something we must learn. Through the grace of God, we can do so. We can learn much from Peter's struggle with a remarkably similar situation.

We have all read the story of Peter walking on the water. It is a brief account of faith, the Lord's word and presence, threatening circumstances, and a man who believed, then feared. He began to sink because of his fears and doubts, and was rescued by the hand of Jesus. Finally, he was questioned by the Lord as to why he had ever doubted, as the seas calmed, and the challenge was over. The account reads as follows: "Jesus made His disciples get into the boat and go before Him to the other side...the boat was now in the middle of the sea, tossed by the waves, for the wind was contrary. Now in the fourth watch of the night Jesus went to them, walking on the sea. And when the disciples saw Him walking on the sea, they were troubled, saying, 'it is a ghost!' And they cried out for fear. But immediately Jesus spoke to them, saying, 'Be of good cheer! It is I; do not be afraid.' And Peter answered Him and said, 'Lord, if it is You, command me to come to You on the water.' So, He said, 'Come.' And when Peter had come down out of the boat, he walked on the water to go to Jesus. But when he saw that the wind was boisterous, he was afraid; and beginning to sink he cried out, saying, 'Lord, save me!' And immediately Jesus stretched out His hand and caught him, and said to him, 'O you of little faith, why did you doubt?' And when they got into the boat, the wind ceased" (Matt. 14:22-32).

This is not a story about a minor miracle that happened to Peter, and has no relevance for us today. On the contrary, the account has tremendous insight for each of us. You see, "walking on the water" is not an option for us - it is required! That is, it is required if we are to live in a place of peace and be sustained by the quiet, deep flow of joy within. Jesus had sent the disciples on before Him. He was directing their path. That path led them into contrary winds and boisterous seas. Jesus then came to them in this situation, walking on the water. How wonderful! The velocity of the wind, and the raging of the seas were no obstacle for Him. He was demonstrating to them that in Him, they could, and should, walk right through apparent difficulties as though they were not there.

That which appeared a hindrance in the natural was, in the realm of the Spirit, no obstacle at all. Jesus made progress over the water in the midst of the boisterous winds and the rough seas. Peter then says to Him, "Okay, Lord. If this is You, I want to do the same thing you are doing. Bid me to come and walk on the water also." In other words, teach me to rise above that which my natural eyes behold and my natural mind comprehends as destruction. As he then stepped out of the boat, we read that "he walked on the water to go to Jesus." It worked! He could walk on the water! Whereas in the natural, the danger of the rough seas was very real and visible, yet because Peter believed the Lord, he began to walk on the water just as if he were on solid ground. The wind was still blowing and the seas tossing the boat, but Peter was able to rise above them.

The wind and waves had no power over him, that is, until he took his eyes off of Jesus and began to fear the wind and waves, and to doubt that he could do what he was doing. Then he began to sink - sink into the darkness of despair, hopelessness, that dark ocean of fear, doubt, torment, and the overwhelming seas that drown our light, strangle our faith and grieve our spirits. Instead of standing in the victory, peace, and joy with Jesus on the top of the waves rejoicing, Peter cried out in panic, "Lord save me!" And yes, the Lord does save us in our cries for help, but our calling is to live higher than that. Our calling is to walk in His power, confident that He does lead us and that in all things we are conquerors. And in all things, we can rejoice in Him and have inner peace. Our calling is to not begin to sink when we feel the strength of opposing winds upon our path and see the roughness and danger that surrounds us. Though the winds of opposition and roughness of the way are real, yet we can rise above them as we keep our eyes upon the Lord and His Word.

What are the winds and waves that have come upon your path? God knows they are there. If we trust Him, and the fact that He leads us always, then contrary winds are nothing to fear. They are not brought to us because of our sin and shortcomings, but by the wisdom of God to teach and strengthen us. It was Jesus's command that led Peter and the others into the contrary winds and rough sea. When we fear the opposing circumstances in our lives, and seek to control and work things out ourselves for our own protection, we miss walking in peace and have no joy. When we trust Him, trust Him with all things contrary, and release the outcome completely into His hands we find peace and our feet are sustained on top of the water. We do not sink into the torment of doubt and fear if we rightly release all things into His control and stop trying to figure everything out for ourselves. We are not trusting God when we struggle with questions of "why is the wind contrary?" and "what if this matter gets worse?" or "what if I lose this or that?" or "what have I done to make this thing happen to me?" We need to proclaim, "Lord, You know why this is contrary, and I trust You and put it into Your hands. The outcome is under Your control, and I trust you. I trust You!" If you have asked God to direct your life, then no matter what may come, you are on God's path. Rest in this fact and peace will flood your heart and mind. Rejoice in the knowledge that He is with you always, and that He knows the why of all that is a mystery to us at the moment.

Romans 8:6 tells us, "For to be carnally minded is death, but to be spiritually minded is life and peace." Fear, doubt and lack of trust will lead us to rely upon our own carnal mind to figure a way out of contrary situations. This leads to the death of peace and joy in our hearts, so confusion and torment enter. Spiritual mindedness says, "God, You are in control of every fair and contrary wind, and I know You make no mistakes in my life. I look forward to how You will use every contrary wind to accomplish Your will and way in me. I trust You fully, and request of You to have Your will in all matters concerning me. You have a purpose for this contrary wind touching me, and I yield to Your purposes, accepting gladly every wind tossed sea as an invitation from You saying, "Come, walk above it with Me."

If we put our thoughts upon the magnitude of the wind, and the size of the wave upon which we have found ourselves tossed, we will surely begin to sink, as did Peter. For in doing this we are failing to trust God. Isaiah's words of drawing water from the wells of salvation with joy, follow his proclamation of "Behold, God is my salvation; I will trust, and not be afraid" (Isaiah 12). It is when we trust that we will find His joy and peace reigning in our hearts.

Though we have trusted God in the past, and found Him to be faithful in helping us and working things out for the good, yet with each new touch of a contrary wind, we must put into practice an attitude of trust. It is not easy. It was not easy for Peter. Jesus was right there, in plain sight. Jesus was on the water. Peter had begun to walk on the water. He was experiencing victory and delight in trusting in the Lord's command to "come." And yet, in an instant, his eyes looked upon the wind, he felt its pressure against his face, and he became afraid. It happened just that fast! We too can begin to sink into doubt, unbelief, and fear, as we for just one moment believe that the contrary wind will destroy us. It will not - provided we keep our minds full of God's Words of promise, provision, protection, and blessing. He is with us always, not only when we feel blessed, but in the times of contrary winds as well. Perhaps even more! We are on His path. Repeat that to yourself when times get tough. "I am on God's path!" As you come to accept this as reality, you will receive His peace and joy. If Paul could find it when beaten, bloody and in prison, then so can we! May the Lord's words to us be not, "O you of little faith, why did you doubt?" but rather "receive my peace and joy, because you did not allow the reality of the thing contrary nor doubt to control your thinking, nor to shake your trust in Me!"

Trust, (walking on the water with Jesus in all things contrary) is a command of God for our good. If we ignore the command to trust, and we fear the storm of contrary wind, and choose to work to preserve ourselves, we disobey His word and reap torment and confusion. This was God's lamentation in Isaiah 48:17-18 when He said, "I am the Lord your God, Who teaches you to profit, Who leads you by the way you should go. Oh, that you had heeded My commandments! Then your peace would have been like a river, and your righteousness like the waves of the sea." His commandment is to trust Him!

There is a lesson to be learned in every circumstance God engineers in our lives. When the lesson is learned, the circumstance changes. After Jesus had taught the disciples about their ability, through faith and trust in Him, to rise above circumstances that were very real and threatening in the natural (walking on the water by faith in Him), He admonished Peter for doubting and looking at the wind instead of at Him. They got into the boat and the wind ceased! Contrary winds are no mistake. God does not make mistakes. If you are His, then there is nothing, I repeat, nothing, that touches you that is not in His plan and purpose. The winds will cease, when the lessons are learned. The quicker we accept His hand in the contrary things that come our way, the quicker our peace is found. It is when we struggle against them, question them, doubt God, murmur and complain that we hinder our own development in the Lord. Trust Him, for He loves you and desires only your good!

GET AHOLD OF THIS AND VICTORY IS ASSURED

Heavenly Father, forgive us for our lack of faith in You and Your promises to us. Give us the strength to trust in You, and to wait for Your promises expectantly. Grant us the patience to endure as You fulfill Your eternal and unseen purposes within our hearts. We pray for the gift of release, that ability to let go of our striving and self-dealing, which will allow us to walk with a light and joyful heart. We pray for spiritual stamina to withstand the assaults of darkness against our souls. And for grace to exhibit love and forgiveness in the face of such attacks. Teach us when to speak and when to be silent, when to confront and when to overlook. These wisdoms dwell within You, and we seek their transfer to our daily expressions. In Jesus's name we pray. Amen.

GOD BRINGS CHALLENGE TO ESTABLISH US, NOT DESTROY US

Saul was chosen to be the first king over Israel, not by men, but by God. God directed Samuel to anoint Saul king. Saul, therefore, was not only chosen to be a child of God as a son of Jacob, but again selected by God from among His people to lead them. God knew who Saul was. God put His Spirit upon Saul to enable him to lead Israel (I Sam. 9-11).

God knows your name. God knows who you are. God has chosen you to be His child, and if you have accepted Jesus as the atonement for your sin, through faith in His blood sacrifice, death and resurrection, you are a child of God. He has put His Spirit within your heart and has made many promises to you. Promises He will in no way fail to keep.

Then, unto the chosen, unto the called, unto the anointed came trouble and challenge. Just a few years into his reign as king, Saul was confronted with a crisis of devastating proportions. Jonathan, Saul's son, had attacked a military post of the Philistines, Israel's enemy. The Philistines heard of this attack and gathered them selves together against Saul and Israel. At this time, we read in I Samuel 13 that Saul's men numbered but a few thousand. Here is what we read of the Philistines who came to fight with Saul and his men: "And the Philistines gathered themselves together to fight with Israel, thirty thousand chariots, and six thousand horsemen, and people as the sand which is on the seashore in multitude." Simple math - Israel was greatly outnumbered! There are times when we feel this same opposition in the Spirit.

Saul had been told by Samuel, who anointed him king, "Seven days shalt thou tarry, till I come to thee, and shew thee what thou shalt do" (I Sam. 10:8 & 13:8). However, Saul was under great pressure. His people were distressed, deserting him, hiding in caves and pits and according to I Sam. 13:15, Saul's men had dwindled to a mere six hundred. Saul waited and waited. The Philistines prepared to attack, but Samuel did not come - that is not until after Saul had disobeyed the command to wait and had offered a sacrifice without Samuel (I Sam. 13:8-9).

It is difficult to wait on God when we face overwhelming circumstances. We, like Saul, are tempted to take things into our own hands, to press forward prematurely and by doing so miss the blessing of God (I Sam. 13:11-12). There is a critical lesson in this story for you and me, a lesson that has eternal ramifications. Samuel told Saul that if Saul had waited, as commanded by God, God would have established Saul's kingdom forever! (See I Sam. 13:13.) There are eternal purposes being fulfilled through everything that touches the life of the believer. We are living a life in the

Spirit, in the eternal, NOW! We are engaged in spiritual warfare, spiritual development, and spiritual life every moment, whether we are conscious of it or not. God is using everything in our lives to accomplish His good work within our hearts for our eternal benefit.

Why had the challenge of the Philistines come to Saul? Samuel said in I Sam. 13:13 that the purpose of God in this challenge was to establish Saul, not destroy him. God never brings testing to destroy us, only to establish us. It is true, as the hymn says, "I only design, thy dross to consume and thy gold to refine." We may temporarily seek to remove ourselves from the consuming of our "dross", but we will pay a price with the currency of eternity. Saul's failure of his seemingly "earthly" challenge had eternal consequences - forever is the establishing in the Spirit that Saul forfeited.

What would have happened if Saul had trusted and waited according to the Word of the Lord? What was God's intended blessing and victory? God proceeded to demonstrate the victory that He had planned for Saul. A victory that was given to Jonathan, his son instead. The Philistine army began to move on its attack plan against Israel. The "spoilers" moved out in three companies planning a three-front attack (verse 17-18) against a band of men who did not even all have weapons of war, but rather farm tools (verses 19-23). In chapter 14 of I Samuel, we read of Jonathan, one man, and his armourbearer, slaughtering twenty Philistine soldiers (verse 14). From the swords of one man and his armourbearer - one small victory - God sent a wave of trembling and confusion, and an earthquake, through the entire army of the enemy that caused the Philistine masses, as strong as they appeared, to "melt away...and they went on beating down one another." The result was a great day of victory for Israel - a victory that should have been Saul's, but was credited to Jonathan instead (I Sam. 14:45). A victory that God has planned for you and me - and it is certain!

In summary, what are the key lessons from this story?

1. Never doubt God is with you. Never fear to trust in God's Word for your guidance and as a blueprint for decision making. Prior to Saul's challenge, God had told Saul, "Do as occasion serves you, for God is with you!" Do not let fear freeze you from acting upon God's Word, and never take matters into your own hands.

2. You are God's child, and He will never forsake you! Samuel told Saul, and all Israel, 'The Lord will not forsake his people for his great name's sake: because it has pleased the Lord to make you, his people." We may feel at times, what in the world could please God about making me His child - but it has pleased Him to do so!

3. Though the "spoilers" may be on the move against us, we can wait, and trust in God's Word regardless of the appearance of the challenge or circumstance.

4. There are eternal purposes being fulfilled in every thing that touches our lives. Let us not forfeit their benefit by acting, or reacting, in the flesh in disobedience to the Holy Spirit and the Word of God.

5. Victory is certain! We must arm ourselves with the knowledge that it may come later than we might choose, but it is certain. Jonathan and his armourbearer proved that.

FOLLOW THE SPIRITUAL RULES FOR ETERNAL REWARDS

Heavenly Father, cause us to focus on those things that are eternal, in the realm of the Spirit. Forgive us for spending so much time concerned over worldly matters, cares and concerns You have said You will take care of anyway. Cause us to walk in faith, free from the burdens that unbelief and doubt laden upon us. We cast upon You every care, and we desire to be abandoned to the agenda of the Holy Spirit and Him alone. Your will be done, in us today. In Jesus's name we pray. Amen.

UPON WHICH PLAYING FIELD ARE WE ATTEMPTING TO SCORE POINTS

In Matthew, chapters five and six, Jesus speaks of many things pertaining to the inner life. He speaks of praying in secret, not doing alms for others to see, and fasting in secret. He tells of God's blessing and reward for those whose hearts, in secret, were pure and right with God, though such rewards may never be acknowledged by others around us. The world rewards outward accomplishment. Therefore, it is a major adjustment in our thinking to place greater value on inner growth in our hearts than on outward visible blessing in our lives. This is a difficult transition. We find it easier to equate God's rewards to the outward manifest blessings of life in this world. If we are healthy, if we are blessed financially, if we are accepted and praised by others, we feel rewarded of God, and we may be, although many times the outward blessings are the result of inner obedience and growth. However, Jesus's teachings were of a different playing field. Not the field of our worldly experience, but the invisible field of the Spirit, and the workings of God in the secret places of men's hearts.

In Luke 6:27-35 and Matthew 5:38-48 we find Jesus explaining how to receive God's rewards for the correct heart attitude and behavior. In Luke 6:35, Jesus tells us that for following His teachings on these matters, "our reward shall be great!" To receive these rewards, we must learn what is expected of us, and understand the rules of the game so to speak. If football players were to play in a baseball game, field goals and touch downs would not score them points. They would receive no rewards for such accomplishments because the rules of the game do not award points for field goals and touchdowns, but rather for runs around the bases. Likewise, we must understand the playing field of the Spirit, lest we be found attempting to score points in a manner that is not recognized as rewardable by God.

On the field of the Spirit, it is always what is going on in our hearts that matters, not what is taking place in the outward of our lives. Jesus's teachings tell us, as believers, that we will have enemies, people who will despitefully use us, persecute us, curse us, smite us, and take from us. While we may not spend much time on these verses, may wish to ignore them or hope to pray them away, they are inescapable. And, in counterpoint to the world, He tells us that in these things our reward will be great! Not because we will see His vengeance on the offenders, but because we will learn to react to all such things in His love (Luke 9:53-56). If we were playing on the field of the world, we would count it rewardable if we defeated our enemies, struck down those who struck us so they could not rise again, recovered with interest all that someone took from us, and punished all who caused us harm. Is this not how the world thinks? Isn't this our flesh reaction to all such events as they touch our lives? If we are honest with ourselves, we know very well the reaction of our flesh to having an enemy. It is to see them dealt with - immediately and severely. God says our victory comes in learning to love them, not in having them destroyed. If our hearts are full of resentment, hatred, or bitterness as a result of unfair treatment, then God is most likely going to leave our enemies in place until we learn what He is trying to teach us on the field of the Spirit - love!

Jesus's words put us on notice that, as His followers, we will experience a multitude of negative things. Think about what He says for a moment. "Love your enemies" cannot be learned without having enemies. That means there will come those who seek our hurt, or our demotion, or come to resist us, fight us, and frustrate our efforts. Yes, they may be used of the devil, but we are commanded to learn to love them, pray for them, and "give them drink" (Romans 12:20-21, Proverbs 25:21-22). There may come those who seek to cheat us out of that which is rightfully ours, those who backbite and speak against us, set us up to manipulate and use us for their own purposes and to our hurt. We must remember which field we are playing on! We are not laying up rewards for outward worldly victory, but for inner heart purity and love.

To these negative messengers we are told to give them love, return blessing for cursing, enter prayer for those who seek to despitefully use us, and to turn the other cheek when we are smitten. And to those who take from us, we are told to ask our goods not again, in other words, we are told to suffer the loss. All of this is in direct opposition to our natural flesh reaction, which is to protect ourselves, recover our losses, and get even with those who have treated us unfairly. It is this natural reaction that God seeks to put to death, so we might behave as His children, following Jesus's example. And this work is accomplished in secret, where God sees and deals with the thoughts and reactions of our hearts. There are no secrets from Him, and the outward is allowed until the inner is acceptable to Him. He wants us to succeed in walking acceptably to Him in the Spirit. If we are upset, miserable, tormented by outward circumstances or people, then there is yet an inner work to be accomplished. When the thoughts and reactions of our hearts come into line with God's Word, then the peace of God prevails within. Such is the reward of those who are in obedience to God in the secret places of the heart.

We are told to "be the children of your Father which is in heaven: for He maketh his sun to rise on the evil and on the good, and sendeth rain on the just and on the unjust" (Matthew 5:45). We are to be the ambassadors of heaven, showing forth God's grace, mercy, forgiveness and love in the face of all manner of evil and darkness. This is not easy! We must adjust our thinking to accommodate the ways of the Spirit. Paul experienced truly little outward worldly blessing, fulfilling much of His life in prison. His life is a good example of the playing field of God. Paul stored up eternal rewards, because he knew he was playing on the field of the Spirit.

God allows us to have enemies in order to teach us to yield self to the death of the cross and to learn to trust Him alone. It is never about what we gain or lose in life, but what we gain in the Spirit, in the likeness of Christ that is important (Luke 12:20-21). Once the Holy Spirit gets ahold of a life, that person will live in defeat and misery until they learn which field they are called to play on. The purpose of perceived negative experiences in the natural is to teach us to keep our eyes on the field of the Spirit. Let God unfold the natural as needed to accomplish his will in the heart. God will seek to break our fascination with everything we are trusting in, other than Him!

Jesus's teachings may look difficult to follow, but He demonstrated the greatness of the reward. Following the most negative treatment possible - rejection, beating, humiliation, crucifixion, and death - He rose from the dead!

The embracing of suffering, and the submitting of all things to God, yielding to His will alone, always leads to walking in the power of the resurrection O Peter 2:23). The greater the perceived or actual loss, the greater the victory!

GOD HAS WRITTEN
US INTO HIS WILL

Heavenly Father, open our eyes to behold the great inheritance You have laid *up for us. You purposed to bless us and have given unto us great* promises. *Teach us to walk* in *them and enjoy the privileges afforded Your children. Forgive us for not entering into the attitude of faith which leads us to Your benefits and blessings. Thank You for our heritage, which* is *not based on our goodness, but upon Your love and mercy. In Jesus's name we pray. Amen.*

THE HERITAGE OF THE SERVANTS
OF THE LORD (ISAIAH 54: 17)

If you are a Christian, then God has written your name in His estate plan, His "last will and testament" so to speak. As a father and mother, or other relative, may write your name in their estate plan, giving to you certain of their assets upon their death, so God has done for every believer. This concept of being an heir in God's plan is important to understand. You see, you and I can do nothing of ourselves to cause another to write us into their will. Each person plans their estate to go to certain people for their own reasons. Some people decide that their blood relatives will share equally in all they possess upon their passing away. God's desire for His estate is along these same lines. All of God's blood relatives, those who have had their sins washed clean by faith in the blood of Jesus, believing in

His resurrection and deity, are considered heirs in God's plan. God plans to share with all His children His entire estate. The Bible says we are heirs of God through Christ (Gal. 4:7). If we are sons of God through faith in Jesus, then we are heirs as well.

Not too long ago, I found my name written in the estate plan of one of my deceased relatives - a relative I had a good relationship with, but at times I know I frustrated. Nevertheless, this person had decided that good or bad, like them or not, each surviving blood relative would receive a share of the estate. Each person listed had nothing to do with the blessing being given them, only that the same blood flowed in their veins. Some had very little contact with this person over the years, and others had quite a lot. Some were liked more than others, and some were quite irritating to the deceased. But each was named, and each shared equally. Each had done absolutely nothing to deserve anything at all. It was the desire of the deceased relative to share in this way.

God has decided that He will share with every believer a portion of His estate. We are heirs of God through Christ. We have done nothing to deserve any portion at all. We cannot earn a larger portion. In fact, we cannot earn any portion at all. The inheritance is given to us, our names being written into the estate plan of God almighty, when we become blood relatives through faith in Jesus's sacrifice on the Cross. When we by faith partake of His body and His blood, we are part of the family of God. It is not by good works that we become eligible, but by faith. Titus 3:5, tells us "Not by works of righteousness which we have done, but according to his mercy he saved us, by the washing of regeneration, and renewing of the Holy Ghost; which he shed on us abundantly through Jesus Christ our Saviour; that being justified by his grace, we should be made heirs according to the hope of eternal life."

If you knew that someone had written you into their will, would you be interested in knowing what they had that might be coming your way? I think so. In fact, you might even wish they would go ahead and share it with you while they were alive. In other words, keep what they might need, and give the rest away now. That way they could watch you be blessed before they died. Sounds like a pretty good idea, doesn't it? Well, God thinks along those same lines. He desires us to step into much of our inheritance now, not waiting for some future date. Because our Testator (deceased relative) Jesus has already died and purchased our inheritance for us, it is ours for the receiving. We need to know what ours is today, so that we might enjoy its fullness.

Scripture speaks of being heirs of salvation (Hebrews 1:14), heirs of life (I Peter 3:5), heirs of righteousness (Heb: 11: 7), heirs of God and joint heirs with Christ (Romans 8:17), and heirs of the Kingdom (James 2:5). Jesus told us that the kingdom of God was within. In other words, it was spiritual in nature, and the way into it was through our faith and by walking in the spirit. Through our increased understanding of the Word of God we will learn more about the kingdom of God and our inheritance. Hebrews 1:2 states that Jesus Christ is the heir of all things. And we are joint heirs with Him. That is quite an estate! The limitless bounty of God, the power of God, the blessing of God, the promises of God, the fullness of Jesus's relationship with the Father are ours to share in today. Are we worthy ourselves of such an inheritance? No. Should feelings of low self-worth stop us from stepping into what God desires for us? No. The promises of God are part of His inheritance for us, and it is His desire that we walk in them with thankful and grateful hearts. This especially holds true when we are aware of our mistakes, sins and weaknesses. Perfecting our flaws is God's work. Their presence in us is not a disqualification from our inheritance, but rather proof of our need to rely upon the Holy Spirit within to change us.

In God's eyes it is as though a Wall Street executive were leaving his office. He has been highly successful financially, but his only son died as a boy. As he goes to his waiting limousine, he spots a homeless beggar, a young man who has hit bottom. The executive is moved with compassion.

He goes to the young man and says, "Come with me, I want to help you." He takes the young man home, cleans him up, gives him the finest clothing and transforms his appearance. The executive goes even further and tells the man that he wishes to adopt him as his son. The young man is overwhelmed and with gratitude accepts. Outwardly the young man looks like the son of a successful executive, but when he speaks, he still sounds like a homeless beggar. His inheritance is certain because his adoption is final and irreversible. However, it will take some time for him to become inwardly what he has already officially become in the eyes of the executive, his son. It is similar with us and God. Our inheritance is sure, and our position as children of God is certain and irreversible, but it takes time for the Holy Spirit to transform every area of our hearts and minds.

God speaks a tremendous promise to us in Isaiah 54:11-17. He is addressing His people who were "afflicted, tossed with tempest, and not comforted." Sometimes we are tossed with doubts of being worthy to receive anything from God. We know in our hearts we deserve nothing. We at times entertain the devil's lies of condemnation as he points out our flaws and shortcomings. But to all of this God has an answer. He is laying a beautiful foundation in our hearts through our struggles (verse 11-12). He is establishing us in the Spirit in righteousness (verse 14). He promises us we will be far from oppression and will not fear. In other words, we will learn to tell the devil to flee, and we will no longer entertain his lies and seeds of doubt and unbelief (verse 14).

We may be challenged from without, and tested from within. God knows about it all. After all, He created even those who seek to destroy (verses 15-16). He promises that no weapon formed against us will prosper, and that every tongue that speaks against us to judge us as wrong or unworthy we will prove to be wrong (verse 17). We will prove every condemning tongue and thought to be wrong for one reason alone. Not because we are good. Not because we don't make mistakes. Not because we do everything perfectly. Not because of our good works. But because

God said so in Isaiah 54: 17 for two powerful reasons. First, this is our heritage...our inheritance. We had nothing to do with it, God said it was ours. And secondly, He secures our justification for receiving His blessings by further stating, "and their righteousness is of me, saith the Lord." Oh, bless His holy name. Our righteousness is of Him. It is His gift to us, and that makes us worthy to receive all of His promises, and the fullness of our inheritance. We will stand against all that may come against us, and we will prevail, because of Him and His decree. He said so. Praise God.

Printed in the United States
by Baker & Taylor Publisher Services